Herding the Ox

The Martial Arts as Moral Metaphor

Herding the Ox

The Martial Arts as Moral Metaphor

by Dr. John J. Donohue

Turtle Press *Hartford*

Herding the Ox: The Martial Arts as Moral Metaphor

To contact the author or order additional copies of this book:
Turtle Press
401 Silas Deane Hwy.
PO Box 290206
Wethersfield, CT 06129-0206
1-800-778-8785

Cover Art by Kathleen Sweeney
Cover Calligraphy by Sang Hwan Kim
Oxherding illustrations reprinted courtesy of Grove/Atlantic, Inc.

ISBN 1-880336-18-9
First Edition
Library of Congress Number 97-49087

Cataloging in Publication data

Donohue, John J. , 1956-
Herding the ox : the martial arts as moral metaphor / by John Donohue
p. cm.
Includes bibliographical references
ISBN 1-880336-18-9
1. Martial arts--Psychological aspects. 2. Martial arts--Moral and ethical aspects. 3. Zen Buddhism and martial arts. I. Title
GV1102.7.P75D66 1998
796.8--dc21 97-49087

Contents

Introduction

People bring different expectations to the same book, so it is probably appropriate that I begin by very clearly expressing what this book is (and what it is not).

It will not help you be a better martial artist if you are really only concerned with physical action. I am as appreciative as anyone when it comes to finely executed technique, but I think of the martial arts as a means to an end. There is a relation between means and ends, but in the martial arts today we seem to neglect the second half of the pair. This book is not about the *how* of martial arts practice, but the *why*.

It is about how the martial arts can help us be better people. Not more physically fit people, or people with better self-defense skills, but better people in the moral sense.

This is serious stuff. There is a widespread acknowledgment that training in the martial arts is serious, but most of this comes from the idea that the activity revolves around fighting and (at least theoretically) matters of life and death. Certainly some of this also springs from the fact that the historical experience of Japanese *samurai* have influenced various martial arts forms. References to life and death abound in feudal Japanese writings about the *bugei* (martial arts) like the *Hagakure*. It has lived on even into modern times in the writings of the famous Japanese writer Mishima Yukio.

But when I maintain that the martial arts are serious, I mean that they are very complex and important activities that require all our effort and attention if they are to be followed correctly.

For the martial arts are, in their most complete sense, spiritual disciplines.

There is, of course, a great deal of lip service given to the martial arts as "ways" to some type of enlightenment. Most practitioners know that the suffix *do* in names like kendo, judo, and karatedo means "way" and implies some spiritual dimension to training. Practitioners of Chinese arts know that Taoist philosophy (*Tao* is the Chinese version of *do*) heavily influenced martial arts theory in the Middle Kingdom. The philosopher Confucius thought the practice of archery was a way to help cultivate a refined human being.

Buddhism is also closely associated with the martial arts. Bodhidharma, who helped introduce Mahayanna Buddhism from India to China, is also the legendary founder of the form of Chinese boxing practiced at the famous Shaolin Temple.

Zen Buddhism has probably had the most widely acknowledged impact on the "martial ways" developed in Japan and known as *budo*. *Samurai* warriors during Japan's feudal era adapted Zen practices to calm their minds. A noted Zen master, Takuan Soho, corresponded with the famous swordsman Yagyu Munenori on the similarities between a Zen mind and the mind of a master swordsman. Takuan's *Fudo Shinmyo Roku* has been extensively quoted in martial arts treatises stretching from the 17th to 20th centuries. A modern martial artist who studied karate in Japan even went so far as to suggest that the art was, in fact, a type of moving Zen.

It is, in fact, the Zen tradition that gives a perspective to this book. In the first place, we should note that the dynamics of Zen practice—the methods of training and the experience that training creates— share so much in common with martial arts training that any student investigating Zen will find striking parallels between activity in the *zendo* and training in the *dojo* (see Chapter 2). But more importantly for my purpose here, Zen Buddhists have also been more successful in pointing out the connection between the impact of training on an individual—the experiential plane—and how that further affects relationships with other people. In the martial arts today, we need to explore the moral dimension of what we do more fully, examining its relationship to spiritual development and its emphasis on moral acts.

But when I refer to this spiritual dimension of the martial arts, I am referring to something that is both similar to and different from the Zen tradition as it is understood by most people.

I don't think you need to be a Zen Buddhist to pursue the martial ways in their most complete sense, although some of Zen's insights can be a tremendous help. I do believe that you must share some of the spiritual seriousness—the austerity—that Zen has in common with others of the world's great religions.

To seriously involve yourself in the martial arts requires a type of focus and emphasis on moral action that most people don't usually associate with Zen. As we will see, this is a misconception. But the popular imagination seems taken with the visual imagery of Zen Buddhists engaged in meditation—the practice known as *zazen*—and the sense that this is a quiet, introspective, and seemingly passive pursuit. Silence and self-examination form part of most spiritual activity, but only part—and the Zen masters knew this.

Modern Americans seem to like the quiet side of Zen, and for good reason. It lets them focus on the how and not the why of the activity. In a nation that celebrates plurality and individual choice, it is also a way of avoiding having to make a commitment. Zen, however, is a form of Buddhism and, as such, is devoted toward creating understanding, compassion, and right living. It is not a way to avoid anything. To be a reflective, compassionate human being whose actions consistently reflect these qualities is a demanding task. It requires fidelity to principles, the acceptance of discipline, and the constant making of moral choices. Twentieth century Americans seem increasingly uncomfortable with this kind of activity.

If so, they shouldn't look to the martial arts to help them remain this way. The whole purpose of the martial arts, to my mind, is to reacquaint people with reflection, discipline, and the necessity for conscious moral choice.

But wait a minute, you object. Isn't Zen practice designed to do away with subject-object distinctions? And by choosing any course of action, aren't we creating more distinctions?

Well, yes and no. In the first place, talking about Zen is extremely difficult if not impossible—it's an experiential, not a logical thing. But when we look at the stories told us about Zen masters, we see that they do, in fact, make evaluations, impose rules, and hold disciples to standards. Zen stories are filled with accounts of teachers grilling their students mercilessly, shouting at them, even striking them as a way to help them toward enlightenment.

I enjoy showing people interested in Zen a video clip of a meditation session in a Zen temple. A priest ghosts up and down the silent rows of mediators until, sensing that a student is not doing what he should, the priest gives the wayward pupil a resounding *THWACK* with a staff he carries for just that purpose.

The Zen priest reminds his pupils that actions have implications. It is something that we should keep in mind as well.

Most Americans don't have a Zen master to guide them. They rely on other things—sometimes religion, sometimes not—to lend coherence to their lives. In the last twenty-five years or so, increasing numbers of people have become interested in non-traditional approaches to inner life, and the martial arts have become popular as vehicles for "enlightenment." There is a healthy openness in this willingness to accept non-Western practices. At the same time, some aspects of the martial arts have proven very seductive to people and, because of this emotive hold, can delude practitioners.

The problem is that training in the martial arts is very gratifying. There are the physical benefits of athletic training, the gratifying experience of skill acquisition, the enhanced sense of self. Basically, we sometimes confuse feeling good with being good. After all, aren't we practicing a martial way? Isn't training somehow related to spiritual development?

In short, we confuse the means with the end. They are related. They are not, however, identical.

People who practice the martial arts like to talk about them as "ways." Part of this comes, as we already mentioned, from the Asian heritage of Taoism and Buddhism, especially Zen (which has heavily influenced Japanese ideas about their different "ways"). The Way, however, is a notoriously nebulous term: it refers to something that transcends normal human experience and, although a simple word, can be put to a variety of uses.

What do people mean when they talk about a martial "way?" It can be a way to spend time, a diversion, a hobby, an avocation. It can be a way to learn to beat other people up, a method of self-defense, or a form of competitive sport. Most any martial artist who describes her practice as a "way," however, would be able to agree that this term implies that her training is a bit more complex than that.

It is not that a martial art practiced as a form of recreation, or self-defense, or sport is not complex. Anyone who has had exposure to training in judo (which, despite the complexity of its founder's vision, has evolved a tremendous sport orientation) staggers away from the mat with a very graphic understanding of just how subtle the physical dynamics of *randori* are. Nor do I mean to say that the martial arts do not have, as part of their nature, aspects of recreation or sport or self-defense. After all, I would hope that anyone who spends years training in a martial arts form takes some enjoyment from the activity and that they recognize that the physical dimensions of training are substantial and have a very real relation to questions of competition and self-defense. What I mean to say is that, while these aspects are part of the martial arts, they do not in themselves completely define them. There is something more to martial arts training, an added dimension, that we very often try to express when we discuss our apprenticeships as following one "way" or another.

Describing a martial art as a martial way implies an extension of principles learned in training into areas we would not normally expect. What this means is that the principles that create such clarity in training are somehow transferred as aids to everyday living, which, as we all know, can be very confusing and complex even at the best of times.

Complexity and confusion, in fact, may be said to be widespread conditions of modern existence. I believe that an important part of what people seek from training in the martial arts is a reduction in confusion, a sense of direction, and a feeling of control over seemingly chaotic and dangerous events. These are relatively profound goals to be pursuing through training in any human activity, but they are extremely important ones in relation to studying the martial arts.

It is tremendously appropriate that people set these types of goals for themselves within the context of martial arts study. For one thing, it reflects a realistic mind set. If people study the martial arts simply because they are looking for ways to physically dominate people, they are, to a large extent, deluding themselves. In trained hands, the techniques of the various martial disciplines can be extremely effective. The techniques, however, are only as good as the person using them. They require years of study and effort to acquire. In addition, if someone is truly concerned about acquiring overwhelmingly effective physical power over another, he or she could use any one of the highly efficient modern technologies (such as firearms) to do so. Besides, the whole point for many martial artists is that the skills acquired are so difficult to acquire (and hence encourage the development of virtues like discipline and commitment), and that training should be undertaken in a mind-set of deadly seriousness that simultaneously hopes never to have to use any of the techniques mastered.

For the mature martial artist, the power acquired through study is not power as it is popularly understood. It is something that aids in the spiritual development of the person and, by extension, makes a contribution to the quality of all human life. While this is a point that seems to be frequently lost in popular depictions of martial artists and the arts themselves, it is nonetheless well-understood by those men and women who endure in their training.

They are not looking to become killing machines. They don't want to kill anyone. Nor do they want to be machines. In fact, what they are looking for is a way to become more fully human; to develop, through overtly physical techniques, a spiritual dimension to their lives.

The pursuit of a martial way can aid us in spiritual development, but only if we consciously pursue this path. Refining our skills will make us better technicians. Only by extending the insights gained through training to the rest of our lives, however, will we become better people.

And this goal is the only one worthy of serious attention.

1. Searching for the Ox

Alone in the wilderness, lost in the jungle, the boy is searching, searching!
The Swelling waters, the far-away mountains, and the unending path;
Exhausted and in despair, he knows not where to go,
He only hears the evening cicadas singing in the maple-woods.
(Suzuki 1960:129)

2. Seeing the Traces

By the Stream and under the trees, scattered are the traces of the lost;
The sweet-scented grasses are growing thick - did he find the way?
However remote over the hills and far away the beast may wander,
His nose reaches up to the heavens and none can conceal it.
(Suzuki 1960:130)

3. Seeing the Ox

On a yonder branch perches a nightingale cheerfully singing;
The sun is warm, and a soothing breeze blows, on the banks the willows are green;
The ox is there all by himself, nowhere is he to hide himself;
The splendid head decorated with stately horns - what painter can reproduce him?
(Suzuki 1960:130)

4. Catching the Ox

With the energy of his whole being, the boy has at last taken hold of the ox;
But how wild his will, how ungovernable his power!
At times he struts up a plateau,
When lo! He is lost again in a misty impenetrable mountain-pass.
(Suzuki 1960:131)

5. Herding the Ox

The boy is not to separate himself with his whip and tether,
Lest the animal should wander away into a world of defilements;
When the ox is properly tended to, he will grow pure and docile;
Without a chain, nothing bidding, he will by himself follow the oxherd.
(Suzuki 1960:131)

6. Coming Home on the Ox's Back

Riding on the animal, he leisurely wends his way home;
Enveloped in the evening mist, how tunefully the flute vanishes away!
Singing a ditty, beating time, his heart is filled with a joy indescribable!
That he is now one of those who know, need it be told?
(Suzuki 1960:132)

7. The Ox Forgotten, Leaving Man Alone

Riding the animal, he is at last back in his home,
Where lo! The ox is no more; the man sits serenely
Though the red sun is high up in the sky, he is still quietly dreaming.
Under a straw-thatched roof are his whip and rope idly lying.
(Suzuki 1960:132)

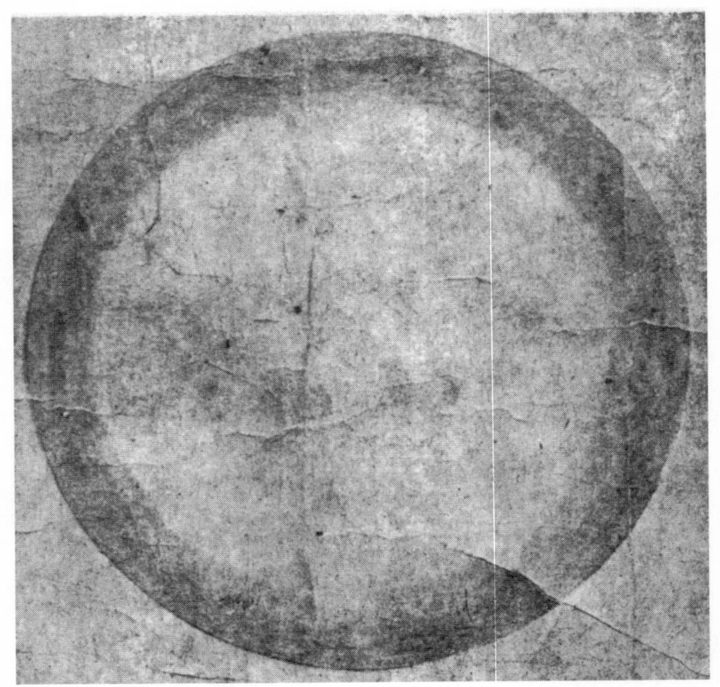

8. The Ox and Man Both Gone Out of Sight

All is empty - the whip, the rope, the man and the ox;
Who can ever survey the vastness of heaven?
Over the furnace burning ablaze, not a flake of snow can fall;
When this state of things obtains, manifest is the spirit of the ancient master.
(Suzuki 1960:133)

9. Returning to the Origin, Back to the Source

To return to the Origin, to be back at the Source - already a false step this!
Far better it is to stay at home, blind an deaf, and without much ado;
Sitting in the hut, he takes no cognisance of things outside,
Behold the streams flowing - whither nobody knows;
and the flowers vividly red - for whom are they?
(Suzuki 1960:134)

10. Entering the City with Bliss-bestowing Hands

Bare-chested and bare-footed, he comes out into the marketplace;
Daubed with mud and ashes, how broadly he smiles!
There is no need for the miraculous power of the gods,
For he touches, and lo! The dead trees are in full bloom.
(Suzuki 1960:134)

2. Herding the Ox, Wielding the Sword

Of training in swordsmanship, D.T. Suzuki wrote
"It was here that the swordsman joined hands with Zen"

The pursuit of any type of spiritual development is often a difficult path. Those who have chosen the martial arts as a vehicle for this quest are, however, immensely fortunate to have an entire corpus of techniques and commentary to help in the pursuit of their humanity.

Yet, despite the fact that an overt linkage between Zen and the martial arts has long been recognized, the specifics of the Zen Buddhist tradition have not been as assiduously mined as a way of discussing the pursuit of the martial arts as spiritual activity. Fortunately, the Zen masters have long utilized a series of woodblock prints to discuss and reflect on the process of seeking enlightenment. The most famous of these prints, the **Ten Oxherding Pictures**, despite discussion in general works on Zen, has never been explicitly utilized as a vehicle for discussing the spiritual dimensions of the martial arts. The chapters that follow will not totally remedy this neglect. They will, however, use them as a springboard to discuss the spiritual stages and insights generated in the pursuit of martial ways and their implications.

Martial artists will often speak about the links between Zen Buddhism and the martial arts. This is inspired in large part by the strong influence Zen had on a number of feudal Japanese swordsmen, the styles they developed, and their enduring influence on the modern martial arts. Even today, practitioners of arts like kendo are noted for their acknowledgment that *ken zen ichi* (the goals of swordsmanship and that of Zen are the same). The philosophical and spiritual aspects of the Japanese martial arts (*budo*) are recognized in theory by even those with only a passing acquaintance with either Japanese culture or the martial arts—indeed, it is often part and parcel of the stereotyped ideas they hold about these "mystical" Asian arts.

There are many contemporary America practitioners, however, who believe that this spiritual dimension is something separate from the arts themselves; it is merely a type of exotic window dressing designed to impress the inexperienced or attract the romantic. These martial artists are reacting in part to the public misunderstandings about the arts. They are also exhibiting (whether they know it or not) the type of contempt that comes with familiarity. In either case, people of this opinion believe that the spiritual dimension can be stripped away to reveal the essence of the various arts. This makes them more "effective." You only have to look at the current explosion of "new" and "rediscovered" styles springing up in storefront *dojo* everywhere to see this mind-set in action. These synthetic arts commonly put forward inflated claims about themselves, such as that they are "the ultimate self-defense art" or "the lost art of the *samurai*," etc.

This is all very impressive, but it is entirely beside the point.

I would argue that to strip away the spiritual essence of the martial arts ultimately destroys their beauty and importance. Even worse, it makes the practice of these arts a type of delusionary exercise doomed to disappointment. This is because I maintain (and not everyone agrees with me) that the martial arts cannot be considered fighting arts in the true sense of the word.[1] They are too ritualized, too specialized for that. They take too long to learn. They are of limited use in a world of high explosives and automatic weapons.

There is, however, an entirely different dimension to martial arts training. This is the ethical and spiritual dimension. While we may agree that training in *budo* acts to develop impressive physical techniques, to hammer out weapons of a type in the heat and sweat of the *dojo*, the real purpose of the martial arts is to forge the spirit.

But perhaps you are not convinced of this essential point. Maybe you believe that training in technique can be separated from this other, more important dimension. Even if you could argue that you can bleed human activity of any ethical dimension (and I emphatically believe that this is not so), I think that the insights of Zen have permeated the fiber of the martial arts to such an extent that even the way we go about training demonstrates the relationship between things of the body and things of the spirit.

In fact, when we approach Zen and the martial arts as disciplines (culturally stylized activities oriented toward certain ends) it becomes readily apparent that the structure and technique of training in Zen and *budo* are very similar. As a way of supporting my contentions about the importance of the *do* aspect in the martial arts, I will briefly explore the intertwined histories of *budo* and Zen. This short glimpse at history will then lead us to consider some of the similarities these two areas of endeavor share in methodology. This is most dramatically revealed in the parallels between the experience and development of the martial artist as he or she undergoes the long apprenticeship of the *dojo* and the very similar experience of the seeker of enlightenment in the Zen temple.

The Ten Oxherding Pictures originated with the Chinese Zen masters of the Sung Dynasty (960-1127), and are a series of illustrations and accompanying verses which are used to depict the stages of Zen discipline. In these pictures, the ox represents the human mind, and the various stages depicted represent the attempt to control the mind, transcend dualism, and reach enlightenment (*satori*), the ultimate goal of Zen and, indeed, of all Buddhism. The Oxherding pictures illustrate stages such as searching for the ox, seeing its traces, actually glimpsing the ox, catching it, herding the ox, coming home on the ox's back, etc. (see Chapter Three). The graphic metaphor of herding a large, sluggish, and unruly animal in the search for enlightenment strikes a familiar chord with anyone who has ever suffered through the early stages of meditative training. It also seems a particularly appropriate metaphor for discussing *budo*. For the individual who has trained in the "moving Zen" of the Japanese martial arts, the image evokes a similar response; I know that as a trainee in many *dojo*, I often felt as stolid, plodding, and dumb as the most recalcitrant of beasts.

The link between Zen and *budo* is not just a thematic or pictorial one. The intersection of the practical with the mystical, the blurring of the split between the sacred and profane, is an idea which finds expression in many Japanese cultural phenomena, including Zen Buddhist approaches to the pursuit of enlightenment and training in the Japanese martial arts. The Japanese see no real difference between the purpose of human activity in the *zendo*, the meditation hall of a Zen monastery, and the *dojo*, or training hall of the martial arts. They are vehicles for essentially similar pursuits—the training and liberation of the human spirit—and, as such, the Japanese view the activities from the same perspective and emphasize similar approaches to training.

Zen has had a powerful impact on the modern martial ways (*budo*) of the Japanese[2]. A great deal of this influence is relatively recent, and has only come to the fore within the twentieth century. Zen certainly influenced the outlook of feudal Japanese warriors during the Kamakura and later eras, but much of the evidence from the primary documents of the martial arts during this period is lacking. This is the result of two things.

In the first place, Japanese religious and philosophical beliefs are highly blended. The Japanese have a positive genius for integrating a whole host of beliefs into life. In many ways, they view the varying philosophies of Asia as different roads to the same destination. The Japanese accept Confucian theory regarding social relations, are married in Shinto ceremonies, and have Buddhist funerals. There is a remarkable openness here that has permitted the Japanese to blend faiths and outlooks so that the distinct boundaries between them are lost. The Zen spirit itself is also extremely self-effacing. A Buddhist sect like Zen that emphasizes a direct transmission of enlightenment outside of the scriptures of Buddhism should not be expected to leave many tracks in the historical annals.

In addition, Zen is demonstrated in the doing. We have to look at the lives of swordsmen (and their writings when available) to see traces of Zen. Zen precepts certainly colored the interpretations of master swordsmen such as Miyamoto Musashi, Yagyu Munenori, and Yamaoka Tesshu[3]. At the same time we have to acknowledge that such influence came with the maturation of the martial arts, after centuries of development and reflection. The central trend in martial training, at least until the Tokugawa era (1600-1868), was not oriented solely around the search for enlightenment, but rather was concerned with the utilization of various supernatural techniques to enhance combat performance (Donohue 1988).

As heirs to the martial arts, we have to constantly struggle against over-romaticizing their past. The arts as we know them today did not spring full blown onto the human stage. They were formed over a long period of time by masters and pupils who brought to their studies all the strengths and frailties of human beings everywhere. The history of the development of the martial arts is informative and can help us come to an understanding of the evolution of these arts into the treasures we have today.

Culture and Context

The Strands of Tradition

Many people have very stereotyped ideas concerning the martial arts, their origins, and the cultures and history which formed them. The *samurai* are cowboys with different weapons; the *ninja* are feudal versions of the Green Berets. These ideas create very vivid images and have spawned a generation of B movie action adventures, but add little to our real understanding. A more accurate historical picture can aid in understanding the nature of the martial arts, since it is often historical experience that invests things with meaning.

There are many different martial arts practiced in the world today, ranging from Korean arts like *taekwondo* to the many schools of Chinese boxing popularized as *kung fu*, etc. Most Americans' exposure to the martial arts, however, has been through Japanese *karate-do* and similar arts. Some, like *kendo*, use weapons (or their symbolic equivalents). Others, like *judo*, normally do not. All these different styles (even the non-Japanese ones) have a certain amount in common, since the histories of these arts, like the histories of these countries, are intertwined. For clarity, however, when I talk about the martial arts, I am referring specifically to the systems developed and refined and modified by the Japanese.[4]

Despite this, we have to acknowledge that China's cultural heritage has had a strong impact on the development of all the countries of East Asia, and their martial art systems as well. There is, for instance, mention of boxing in Chinese literature as early as the Chou Dynasty in the *Book of Rites*, as well as in the *Spring and Autumn Annals* (which deals with period between 722-481 B.C.) The technical development of what is known in China as *ch'uan* (or fist) methods was paralleled by the development of the Chinese religious and philosophical system of Taoism. Taoists sought to align their actions with the Way (Tao) of the universe, utilizing *ch'i*, or natural force, as a mechanism for attaining a unity with Nature. There are a number of references in Taoist classics like the *Tao Te Ching* and the *Chuang Tzu* which emphasize the role of breathing exercises in the concentration of *ch'i*. Some consider these statements to be directly linked to physical culture, but most scholars maintain that these references were originally purely philosophical in nature. Nonetheless, in later times boxing was often taught in conjunction with physical and spiritual theories based on Taoism, and in the popular imagination fighting arts became inseparably linked with ideas concerning spiritual development and magic.

There is an additional link between spiritual ideas and combat techniques in East Asia, since Bodhidharma, traditionally identified as the founder of Ch'an (Zen) Buddhism in China, was said to have introduced *ch'uan*-like techniques to the monks he was training in China during the sixth century A.D.

Bodhidharma, a severe taskmaster, was appalled at the lack of physical fitness of the monks he taught, demonstrated by their inability to endure (or even stay awake during) the marathon meditation sessions he instituted. As a remedy to their poor physical condition, it is related that he developed the forms of boxing said to be preserved by the monks of the famous Shaolin Temple. Whether this is history or merely an apocryphal tradition, however, such a story merely serves to underscore the hoary association of fighting arts with philosophical systems.

A host of Chinese cultural factors were to spread across East Asia. The Japanese, while obviously influenced by Chiba, had a rich and well-developed martial tradition of their own. Beginning in the tenth century A.D. local magnates in Japan were increasingly dependent on bodies of armed retainers—the *samurai*—for the preservation and consolidation of political power. The Japanese had initially attempted to establish an Imperial political system based on that of China, but it rapidly succumbed to the regional interests and ambitions of powerful local families. The warriors, or *bushi*, of medieval Japan soon became the dominant political force, and assumed direct political control over the destiny of that country with the establishment of the Kamakura Shogunate in the twelfth century. Various military dictators (*shogun*) would seize control in the tumultuous centuries of Japan's feudal era, and in this violent and unstable age there was an understandable refinement of combat techniques and systems.

The Japanese developed a wide variety of martial techniques (*bujutsu*) for a number of weapons. Prominent among these were *kenjutsu* (swordsmanship), *sojutsu* (the art of the spear), and *kyujutsu* (archery). Many of these techniques were codified into schools or styles known as *ryu*. The mastering of a martial art was an indispensable achievement for the dominant social class, since the *samurai*'s exalted social position was symbolized by the wearing of two swords.

Japan was unified in 1600 by Tokugawa Ieyasu, who ended a period of civil war and established a stable feudal government which endured until the Meiji Restoration of 1868. This outbreak of peace meant that the traditional arts of the warrior were no longer needed in a practical sense. There was a subsequent marked increase in practicing these arts for their moral and spiritual utility rather than their military use. Training in these systems was seen as part of what constituted the activity of a refined individual and these arts came to be understood not simply as techniques (*jutsu*) but as martial "ways" (*budo*) which could lead to spiritual development. Even after the modernization of Japan in 1868, these arts were still practiced, both as ways of preserving traditional culture and as vehicles for spiritual development. The late nineteenth and early twentieth centuries witnessed the development of a number of martial ways (such as *judo* and *kendo*) which had their origins in overtly combative systems, but which had been modified to make practice safer.

Magic and Morals

One of the characteristics that tend to make the Asian martial arts unique is the rich philosophical system associated with them. The various forms of Japanese *budo* share this tradition.

The strands of the belief system that developed as part of the practice of military arts in Japan can be understood as being initially composed of two dominant themes: a curiously pragmatic yet mystical element concerned with the magical enhancement of fighting skills; and an ethical element concerned with a code of honor and behavior, which developed out of the philosophy that served as a guide for moral behavior by the warriors of Japan. As the philosophy of these arts evolved, a third strand would eventually be formed: one which used the systemic training in martial techniques (previously put to use for political ends) as a road to personal development and spiritual fulfillment.

The mystical side of the feudal Japanese martial arts was concerned with practices that could increase a warrior's fighting ability. Ideas about the mystical components to combat in Japan developed from popular interpretations of beliefs imported there from China. Taoist, Yin-Yang, and Five Element philosophies all speculated on ways in which human beings could more closely integrate themselves with the forces inherent in nature. Warriors speculated that these same forces could be used in a type of "applied mysticism" for their very specific purposes. Unlike the case in modern *budo*, where a significant spiritual dimension is dominant, the importance of these beliefs for feudal warriors was that they were thought to offer the fighter an actual "edge" which could make all the difference in combat.

This may strike the modern reader as a perversion of philosophy. We must be careful, though, never to idealize the development of the martial arts. The people who developed and passed on these arts were extremely results-oriented, and the results they were interested in were violent ones. A Japanese warrior traditionally thought that he had about one chance in three of surviving a battle. If his opponent had superior skills, the warrior would die. Due to the extreme sharpness of the *katana* (the long sword), the *bushi* also assumed that an even match would probably result in both parties dying from wounds received in the contest. Only if the warrior could apply truly superior technique did he have the slightest chance of surviving. It was therefore the promise of an animated sword, not an enlightened mind, that first attracted *samurai* to consider a mystical dimension to fighting.

Various philosophies contributed toward the belief in *ki* (force) we find in the modern martial arts. Despite different degrees of intellectual emphasis and technical interpretation, most Japanese martial arts can be seen, in part, as a type of physically expressed dialogue on the question of *ki*. The concept of *ki* is present today in arts such as kendo and karate, and it is of an obviously central importance in an art like *aikido*, where the very name of this martial art translates as the "way of harmonizing *ki*."

Yin/Yang and Taoist beliefs concerning the role of power and weakness are preserved in sayings such as "to yield is to be preserved whole" and the concept that "weakness overcomes hardness, softness overcomes strength" that are handed down in *dojo* today. These ideas have had an obvious impact on the development of empty-hand systems such as *judo*, *jujutsu*, and *aikido*.

Masters of swordsmanship have long stressed ideas from Yin/Yang and Five Elements throughout in their art. Miyamoto Musashi, who wrote a classic treatise on swordsmanship known as the *Book of Five Rings (Go Rin No Sho)* late in the seventeenth century divided his work into sections entitled Earth, Water, Fire, Wind, and Void (a Japanese variation on the Chinese categories of earth, water, fire, wood, and metal—the Five Elements). This reflects a belief that an awareness of the various properties associated with these elements could enhance a warrior's performance.

At the same time that the *bushi* in feudal Japan were exploring ways of enhancing their combat abilities, they were also contemplating their role in the social and political life of their era. As early as the twelfth century, we note the development of concepts concerning the need for honesty and loyalty on the part of the armed retainers of provincial lords. This stress on fealty to one's lord was, in essence, the main thrust of the evolving ethical code of the *bushi*. That this quality of loyalty was so strongly emphasized points to the fact that the ideals of the stalwart, courageous, and loyal warrior were forms of behavior only sporadically lived up to. In fact, the annals of feudal Japan are filled with tales of treachery, desertion, and the seeking of personal gain. It was really only with the centralized feudalism of the Tokugawa shogunate that firm lines of political allegiance were established as a guide to behavior on the part of the warrior.

Although the idea that *bushi* should be courageous, loyal, generous, and socially responsible was for some time an undercurrent in the serious thinking feudal warriors did about their trade, it was not until the Tokugawa Era that the major works on a code of ethical behavior for the *bushi* were written. The *Buke Sho Hatto* (Rules for Martial Families) of the Tokugawa House are an example of this evolving ethical code, since they served as the model for all *bushi* throughout Japan. This work stressed, not surprisingly, absolute loyalty to the *shogun* and emphasized the need for the warrior to behave in a moral and socially responsible manner.

The *Hagakure*[5] was an eighteenth century work written in much the same spirit as the *Buke Sho Hatto*. Often cited for its encouragement of *bushi* to transcend thoughts of life and death, a closer examination shows it to reflect the growing awareness of the need for a moral code on the part of the *samurai*: "We will be second to none in the performance of our duty. We will make ourselves useful to our superiors. We will be dutiful to our parents. We will attain greatness in charity" (Draeger 1974:31).

This is an essentially Confucian world-view, and one very well suited to the martial arts. Confucianism has always stressed the importance of proper relationships between superiors and inferiors in a social environment. It should come as no surprise that a type of Confucianism emerged as the official philosophy of the Tokugawa *shogunate*. This philosophy stressed moral intuition, an innate sense of the good, and social activism. As such, it fit nicely with the political requirements of the Tokugawa government and was at least partially inspired by philosophical systems and activist sentiments that the *bushi* were familiar with.

Confucianism is nothing if not complex, however. In addition to ideas concerning social obligations, it is also a philosophy that emphasizes self-cultivation and rectitude as a way to cure the world's ills. Confucianism, which had evolved for a millennium on the Chinese mainland before influencing the Japanese, fostered a respect for learning and the development of skill, and maintained that the "superior man" had an obligation to serve society, exhibiting wisdom and benevolence.

Benevolence, in fact, seemed to be in the air. The unification of Japan in the seventeenth century had also reduced the need for a large standing body of fighting men. From this period on, we note the encouragement of the pursuit of the more gentle arts by the *samurai*, a development that also had an impact on the martial arts. The support of the ruling house for a Neo-Confucian philosophy, combined with a declining martial emphasis, encouraged the transformation of purely combat-oriented techniques into ways for spiritual and moral development.

This aspect of martial training had been evolving for some time, of course. Rapidly moving political and social events in Japan, the pacification of the country, the development of a conscript army after the Meiji Restoration of 1868, and the final abolition of the samurai class after 1876 combined with the continuing emphasis on Confucianism, encouraged the evolution of *budo* into its present form: that of a physical system geared not towards combat training but toward moral development.

Martial artists, in other words, began to become more introspective about their practices. Once again, mystical concepts were increasingly linked with training. These concepts were ready at hand due to a long historical association between Zen Buddhism and the *samurai*. This Buddhist sect grew in influence in Japan during the twelfth century A.D., at the same time that the *samurai* emerged as a class of armed retainers who would have a substantial impact on Japanese political life and on the development of the martial arts.

Zen claims these four characteristics: a special transmission outside Buddhist scriptures; an absence of dependence on words or letters; direct concern with the true nature of man; and an emphasis on the ability to see into one's true nature and attain Buddhahood. Zen's emphasis on the attainment of mystical enlightenment (*satori*)—an intuitive grasp of, or unity with, the One--coupled with its simplicity, was a highly attractive philosophy for the warriors of feudal Japan, since, in Suzuki's words "Zen appeals to the facts of life instead of concepts" (Barrett 1956:288).

The attraction of Zen for warriors was in its direct appeal to the experience of life, its independent nature, and a related idea concerning the unity of life and death. These were many of the same qualities valued by fighting men in feudal Japan. The mental discipline of Zen, which was thought to generate these qualities, consequently came to play a prominent part in the training of the *bushi*.

Zen has had an immense impact on Japanese culture in general, of course, but the direct utilization of Zen disciplines such as *zazen* (meditative sitting) in martial training points to a firm belief by the *bushi* in the beneficial results associated with the practice of Zen. Here again, however, there was a strong practical theme in the adaptation of philosophy to the martial arts during the feudal period. While not discounting the profound philosophical nature of Zen, we may conclude that, for all but the most exceptional martial artists in any era, the side effects of Zen, the calmness of mind and related speed of reaction time, assumed an importance greater than the attainment of enlightenment. It was only with the fading of a practical use for the martial arts that the philosophical aspect came to be more strongly emphasized.

What martial artists have sought through *zazen* was no separation between them and their art, no hesitation between thought and deed. As with Taoism and other philosophical systems incorporated into the belief system surrounding the martial arts, Zen-influenced ideas pointed to yet another way for martial artists to enhance skill: a way of perception that accelerated reflex action. Thus, the practice of *zazen* became an integral part of training in all Japanese martial arts for centuries and continues to do so to this day.

This dimension was a timely development for the martial arts. We have noted a strong thread of pragmatism in Japanese approaches to the techniques of self-defense. With the advent of the modern era in Japan, traditional forms of combat were displaced by those based on Western technology. Japanese warriors were nothing if not realists; their profession demanded it. It was inevitable that, if traditional martial arts were to survive, that they develop a different rationale for their continued practice.

A more spiritual aspect to martial arts practice consequently began to be emphasized. The vocabulary and philosophy of Zen found a home in the precincts of *budo dojo*. Training here was reinterpreted as a way to self-realization and enlightenment. The incorporation of *zazen* in martial training led to the current synthesis in modern martial arts where it became very difficult to say whether Zen served to improve *budo* or whether *budo* was really "moving Zen" (see Nicol 1975).

In retrospect, we see that the martial arts are cultural systems subject to reinterpretation according to the needs of human beings in different times and different places. For ancient Chinese, Okinawan, and Japanese warriors, martial arts were practical systems dealing with the hard business of killing and being killed. Their primary emphasis was on efficacy. The emerging complexity of martial arts forms and the ideas surrounding them reflects the many-faceted nature of human life: all people, even the most practical, speculate on questions of ultimate meaning and spiritual development. In feudal Japan, esoteric beliefs satisfied not only this human hunger for "deep meaning," but were also thought to have a favorable impact on martial skill. In the case of these arts, fighting skill developed along with philosophical speculation.

The introduction of Western science and technology in the East highlighted another dimension of the martial arts. No serious martial artist would ever maintain that archaic fighting arts are more effective than the technology of modern warfare. They rather emphasized the cultural aspect of martial arts practice, in terms of its ability to teach socially-sanctioned values.

The problem here is that, as cultural systems, the martial arts are themselves tools of human agents. They can be used or abused by individuals. In absolute terms, there is no moral taint (or moral benefit) in the practice of the martial arts; historical circumstance and individual predispositions determine to what ends they will be used. This was made abundantly clear during the first half of the twentieth century in Japan.

As a result, the martial arts in Japan entered another phase of reinterpretation at the close of the Second World War. The more philosophical, ethical, and peaceful aspects of their philosophies came to the fore. As arts of "self-defense" they were rehabilitated in the world's view, and made to serve a variety of functions in the modern world.

A summation of the development of the philosophy behind the martial arts, while filled with the dangers generalization always brings, is nonetheless instructive. This philosophy has its foundation in metaphysical ideas dealing simply with the interpretation of natural phenomena and the isolation of principles that affect life in the world. These insights were then harnessed in a program devoted to the direct application of these principles to systems designed to boost fighting skills. Only much later, when the need for combat efficiency had declined, did the ideas surrounding the martial arts begin to be interpreted in different ways. Like all ideological and philosophical systems, that of *budo* is flexible and may used for good or evil, for political ends or for spiritual development.

This presents a challenge to martial artists today. It is up to them to decide how they will utilize the fruits of centuries of evolution; whether they will view the current practice of *budo* as a thing of the spirit, developed after long, painful, and sometimes erroneous development into something elevating and positive, or whether their interpretation of the arts will regress into a vision of the celebration of pain and animal force.

Certainly the testimony of many wise and accomplished martial artists indicates that, at their best, these arts are a way to liberate us from the dark, bloody world of violence and confusion. In many ways, it became apparent to a host of martial artists throughout Japanese history that, at best, the martial arts were means to a type of end that would eventually make the arts themselves meaningless. These masters testify that there is a spiritual dimension to the arts.

The Japanese martial arts, then, are the product of centuries of refinement in its most all-encompassing sense. They make an overt statement about the connection between body and spirit. The practitioners of these arts most emphatically state, in verbal teaching and compelling physical demonstration, and using the type of contradiction and complexity that seems to characterize life's experiences, that training in archaic techniques of violence can lead to an authentic, fully humane life in the here and now.

And that by losing ourselves in the pursuit of such arts we ultimately find our true nature.

This brief history shows us, in fact, that there has been so much interplay between philosophy and technique in the development of the martial arts that a denial of the relationship seems simple-minded. You can debate whether or not the similarities in Zen and the martial arts are the result of the fact that Buddhism shaped *budo*, but that is, to a point, beside the fact for martial artists today. In a sense, both Zen and *budo* were shaped in the same cultural matrix. Unlike that of the West, the Japanese approach to exalting the human potential of either the spirit or the body is conceived of without any kind of material/spiritual split. Thus there is a unity of technique and characteristics which may be found in activities as seemingly disparate as "herding the ox" or wielding the sword. This is because martial artists came to believe, in a sense, that they are ultimately about the same things.

Themes in Training

Let's acknowledge that *budo* and Zen share similar approaches because they are ultimately striving toward the same goal. The first thing we find is a common emphasis on technique as a means for achieving certain ends. Whatever the popular perception of the process of discipleship among Zen monks or martial artists, my experience in a *dojo* and my readings on Zen training seem very similar. The process of discipleship is an austere one. Training in both disciplines is relentless, and composed of equal parts monotony and physical and mental discomfort, with a dash of terror thrown in.

Technique

The simple repetition of techniques in the *budo dojo*, for example, is thought to be the vehicle which will bring one to mastery. There is little explanation of significance, or even detailed analysis of the mechanics of a technique or the theory that supports it. By concentrating totally on the action, by continuing that action up to and beyond the point of exhaustion, it is thought that the trainee will lose him- or herself in movement. This will make the action a "natural" one, and invests it with a speed, grace and focus which is absent as long as the trainee maintains the distinction between thinking and doing, between himself and the art.

In the art of *kendo*, for instance, the repetition of basic strokes known as *suburi* can in many ways be seen as the moving version of *zazen*. The difficulty involved in performing the movements correctly time after time, and of letting no stray thoughts intrude to break the concentration is analogous to the experience of *zazen*. In this Zen activity of meditative sitting the individual attempts to quiet the mind, to let thoughts come and go as they please until they bubble off, leaving the mind clear. This emphasis on relentless physical and mental training and an appreciation of the ultimate effect of such an activity on the interior state of the individual is reminiscent of the approach of the Soto Zen sect, which stresses the culminating effect of *zazen* over long periods of time. My experience in meditation has shown me that the mind can be as stiff, as unruly, as recalcitrant as the body when one attempts to bring it to a "natural" and spontaneous state.

The heavy emphasis martial arts typically place on training through *kata* (highly stylized, immutable sequences of techniques) is also designed to bring about the same ends. Although more dynamic than the monotonous repetition of *waza* (technique), *kata* have also been compared by Zen teachers to the verbal puzzles known as *koan*: they are both exercises with specific "themes" which underlie a single, central principle.

The close link in the Japanese mind between *zazen* and martial training techniques like *suburi* is dramatized by the training methods employed by Yamaoka Tesshu, the Meiji-era swordsman whose devotion to Zen colored the nature of modern *kendo*. Tesshu was convinced, by reason of his very personal experience of Zen enlightenment, that training in the way of the sword was an intensely spiritual thing. In his *dojo*, known as the Shumpukan, Tesshu initiated an onerous course of study calculated to exhaust the swordsman physically, and to develop an extremely clear and focused mind. So strongly did Tesshu believe that true swordsmanship was a thing of the mind and not of the sword, that he established his own *ryu*, or system, the Muto (No Sword) Ryu.

At the Shumpukan, there was little or no emphasis on explanation or analysis of technique. Novice swordsmen devoted their time to *uchikomi* (a repetitive type of attack training quite similar to *suburi*) for at least three years, a fatiguing and extremely boring apprenticeship. Tesshu thought that such training served to both strengthen the body and focus the mind, imprinting the fundamental techniques on the minds of beginners. Critics of Tesshu's system thought this extreme emphasis on repetition to be foolish and contemptuously termed the training "wood chopping" (Stevens 1984:22).

Even today, students in more traditional arts are struck by the absence of discussion and philosophical reflection in the *dojo*. The emphasis is quite pointedly one on no-frills basics and hard training. Students in such styles are often viewed critically by outsiders for the strict, seemingly pointless type of training regimens they endure. More modern, syncretic systems will stress more of a free-flowing approach to training and disparage *kata*. While such a view may indicate a disappointing lack of understanding of the martial arts, Tesshu's experience demonstrates that, at the very least, such myopia is not a strictly modern phenomenon.

Perhaps the most dramatic training technique Tesshu instituted was that of the *seigan* (a Buddhist term meaning vow). This training technique was one in which a swordsman first completed one thousand days of successive training, and then was required to stand and continuously face two hundred opponents. If this *seigan* was successfully completed, the student was eligible, after further training, to undergo a three day, six hundred match *seigan*. The next and highest level was that of the seven day, fourteen hundred match *seigan* (Stevens 1984:24-25).[6]

The motivation behind such a brutal training method was to truly consume all of a trainee's physical stamina, to wear down his body and exhaust his technique, until the only thing that could compel him to rise for yet another in a seemingly endless series of matches is the power of the spirit. In Tesshu's words, swordsmanship, and particularly *seigan*, "should lead to the heart of things, where one can directly confront life and death" (Stevens 1984:25).

Action, Not Words

Given the high level of repetition and predictability in such training, it is also interesting to note that both Zen and the martial arts do in a seemingly contradictory way also place a very strong emphasis on spontaneity, and frequently rely on sudden strong and often violent actions to propel the trainee into enlightenment. In short, both emphasize the importance of experience, of the potential immanent in the moment, and often rely on the unexpected to shock the trainee into awareness. Thus, in both Zen and *budo*, the trainee must often be subjected to dramatic action to realize his goals.

Certainly the unpredictably of Zen masters is legendary. In one story, a pupil asks his master "What is the basic idea of the Law preached by the Buddha?" The master lifts his swatter; the monk shouts and the master shouts back. The student is left puzzled by this turn of events and the master beats him. In another tale, a Zen monks meets three travellers on a bridge over a river. One asks the monk, "How deep is the river of Zen?" He replies "Find out for yourself" and attempts to throw the traveller into the river. What these anecdotes illustrate is not some cruel streak in Zen training, but rather the conviction that something sudden, unexpected, even painful is sometimes necessary to break the boundaries of normal perception and bring the trainee to a higher plane.

Budo sensei share both this conviction and this unpredictable, confusing style of behavior. They, too, possess the Zen master's insight into something which defies logical expression or rational thought. The attempt by an instructor to articulate an insight which must be experienced often leads the trainee to a profound state of confusion. "Don't think - just do it" my *sensei* would tell me, "but remember not to move your head so much." Or another time: "Go fast! But don't rush." Such admonitions can bring trainees to the brink of despair. Like the Zen *koan*, the advice and maxims of the instructor seek to exhaust the questioner in self-reflection on statements which seemingly have no place in the world as the trainee understands it—certainly the sound of one hand clapping is only heard in *dojo* where the swordsmen go fast but don't rush.

The ultimate experience of confusion for the martial artist is not *koan*, but combat. The experience of engaging in a contest match with your instructor is as dramatic, frightening, and potentially painful as the *mondo* (question and answer session) with the Zen master who beats you for foolish answers or offers to drop you into a river. *Kendo*, for instance, comes alive and has meaning in the experience of practice matches (*keiko* or *jiyu-renshu*). The opportunity to engage in *keiko* with one's *sensei* is an occasion which is both anticipated and dreaded. Here the instructor attempts to elicit the best from the pupil, to push the trainee to the limits of skill and endurance, and sometimes beyond them. Although *kendo* is practiced with bamboo staves and protective armor, there is nothing so deadly serious, so intimidating, as engaging in a match with a *kendo sensei*. The heated clash and thrust of this combat burns away all illusion and pretense on the trainee's part, and graphically illustrates how well or how poorly the lessons of the *dojo* have been learned.

Outsiders are continually told that to understand *budo* you must actually do *budo*. To read about, to ponder a martial art does little or nothing to prepare you for the experience of practicing it. Trevor Leggett, an accomplished *judoka* and writer on Zen, notes that to read about Zen and its relation to Japanese arts "...without practicing a field of a way may be annoying as well as fruitless" (1978:118). Only in the practice of such an art does the link between *budo* and Zen become apparent. In *kendo*, for instance, once you take up the *shinai* (bamboo foil) in contest, there is no time for thought or reflection. You are immersed in a swift moving current of events which, like the search for *satori* (enlightenment) demands a focus on and attention to the now that is as exhilarating as it is disconcerting.

Discipline

Finally, both disciplines stress the importance of a master-disciple link, of authentication of experience through pedigree, of an almost mystical transmission of insight through *roshi* or *sensei*.

The unchallenged primacy of the martial arts *sensei* is one of the most distinguishing features of the traditional Japanese *dojo* (see Donohue 1990). The importance of the *sensei*, who occupies the pinnacle of the ranked society of the *dojo*, cannot be overstated. The primacy of the master over his disciples bears with it not only connotations of technical mastery, but of moral and spiritual authority as well.

The position of the *sensei* is analogous to that of the Zen *roshi* who leads a disciple to enlightenment through *mondo*, the posing of *koan*, and supervision in the discipline of Zen. The position of the *sensei* is also stressed due to the belief that the transmission of skill and insight in the martial arts can only be obtained from a recognized teacher who stands at the end of a direct chain of master-disciple relationships which stretches from the time of the style's founder into the present. We can compare this concern with pedigree to the Zen concern with the transmission of insight through the early patriarchs[7] and the authentication of enlightenment required in Zen today.

Like Zen, there is a very real sense of spiritual transmission in *budo*. This is partly the result of the fact that the founders of various martial arts schools or styles were very often charismatic individuals who were considered to have had a flash of inspiration or enlightenment which led to their prominence in *budo*. The very personal experience of study in Zen or a martial art under the direction of a master whose technical and spiritual superiority completely dominates the physical and psychological states of the novice during his training serves to perpetuate this sense of mystical transmission of skill and/or insight.

Both Zen and martial arts like *kendo* challenge the trainee, and shape the student through a number of similar paradigms. They are, in a sense and on the surface, very different disciplines; one seems to be about the training of the mind, the other about the training of the body. Since, however, they share similar goals—the creation of an unclouded vision of the here and now—they have also adopted similar techniques. Both acknowledge the fact that somehow human culture has impaired our perception of the world. They are both fundamentally optimistic in their assessment of the situation, however, for they both maintain that through training, persistence, and effort, this faulty perception may be rectified. These two disciplines acknowledge, at least implicitly, the fact that culture is both an occasion of danger and an occasion of enlightenment in the human experience.

So, how "real" is the link between Zen and *budo*? There is no argument concerning the essentially spiritual nature of Zen. Those, however, who have trained in the martial arts, have experienced their rigors in training and are simultaneously aware of the martial arts growing sport and tournament orientation may question whether these arts can truly be considered true *Do*, ways or paths to enlightenment. Our historical survey reveals that they were originally activities used for vastly different purposes. Even the way in which spiritual doctrines have been interpreted has varied with time. The answer to the question, of course, is that these arts are what we choose to make them. The link is strong only if we act to forge it that way.

We shouldn't shrink from that task. I think that our doubts about the identity of the martial arts as true "ways" is the result of how we have been conditioned to view a fundamental split between the physical and the spiritual in the West. This doubt says more about our preconceptions regarding the physical and the spiritual than it does about these categories themselves. Certainly the idea of the mutually exclusive nature of these categories is a concept that proponents of Zen and the martial arts do not consider valid.

Kendo, for example, has a long pedigree in the Japanese martial tradition and has a well-established link with Zen. It is also relentlessly competitive and has extremely strong sport overtones in modern Japan. Yet *kendo* players all over the world consider it to be vested with a transcendent significance. The merging of things of the flesh and things of the spirit in *kendo* and can be understood as emblematic of all the martial arts.

Consider the atmosphere of a *kendo dojo*, which I recounted in another work:

> The *taiko*, the great drum, boomed, calling the class to order. Fifty *kendoka* silently knelt in a line stretching down the length of the *dojo*. Only the dry rasp of calloused soles along the hard wood floor and the swish of uniforms could be heard. The seated bow was performed. The basic exercises were performed efficiently. A type of reserve was exhibited at all times. . .
>
> . . .The effect was one of timelessness. As they put on their equipment the *kendoka* also put on the tradition of *kendo*; its form, its purpose. They surrendered individuality and became one with the art of the sword. . .

. . .In the silence of that hall, the *sensei* signalled with the hollow tap of two blocks of wood that free practice was to begin. Before that sound had faded, each *kendoka* had joined in furious combat with an opponent. . . The clatter of *shinai* striking armor, in itself overwhelming, was overcome by the force of the cries emanating from these combatants. These *kiai*, the shouts common in many martial arts forms, had an incredible emotional impact. I had always understood *kiai* to be a symbolic sound used to express the martial artist's single-minded purpose, the unity of spirit and technique.

To hear *kiai* in the kendo *dojo*, however, was to experience it not as a mere symbolic expression of that condition, but as its palpable reality. I was familiar with the contention of some Zen masters that a shout could, in some cases, actually propel a student into *satori*. . .The *kiai* of the *kendoka* that day had a similar quality and impact which, as an analytical observer of *budo*, I was somewhat at a loss to explain.

There is an old adage used (and perhaps over-used) in Zen and the martial arts, to the effect that when you first see a mountain, it is just a mountain. Later, after training, you realize that it is not just a mountain, it is something more. Finally when you reach an enlightened state, you realize once more that the mountain is just a mountain. This hints at the fact that the Zen "beginner's mind" is often much closer to the proper perception of reality than we realize.

I like to think that what I observed and felt that first day in the kendo *dojo* was, in some ways, an accurate insight into this discipline. . .

> The enduring image I have of kendo is not the flash of technique or the sweat of effort. Instead, I hear the boom of the drum; see the silent row of swordsmen bow and, with the dull summons of wood blocks, join together in a mysterious struggle whose real goal is the liberation of the human spirit (Donohue 1992).

In other words, while it may be possible to practice the martial arts without a Zen-influenced perspective, the overtly ethical and transcendental components of Zen may be indispensable for modern practitioners looking to pursue a martial "way."

What we witness in truly realized martial arts training, then, is a fusion of body and spirit. Through training, we become different people, men and women with enhanced abilities and strengthened senses of purpose.

The uninitiated may believe that, on reaching this state, we have achieved the ultimate goal. Both Zen and martial arts masters, however, would suggest that we still have some distance to go.

In other words, now that we have attained this skill, what do we do with it? Where do we go from here? What is the ultimate point? These are the last, hard questions that martial artists so frequently ignore and yet need so desperately to be answered. We may have thought that training was difficult and arduous. The starkness of these final questions reveals that this was all prelude to the more significant challenge that lays ahead. In this regard, we need to turn to the insights generated from the Oxherding Pictures to see if they can aid us in the continuing journey in the martial ways.

Note for Chapter Two

[1] Readers who are interested in following the development of my particular argument can take a look at my "Martial Systems: A Cross-Cultural Typology" in the *Journal of Asian Martial Arts*, as well as my book *Warrior Dreams: The Martial Arts and the America Imagination*.

[2] Interested readers can see the works by Suzuki (959) and Leggett (1978).

[3] See Victor Harris' translation of the *Go Rin No Sho* (1974), Sato's work on the Yagyu *Heihokadensho* (1985), and John Steven's biography of Tesshu (1984).

[4] This limitation does not reflect my lack of appreciation of the martial arts of other countries—particularly the complex body of arts from China. It is really only the product of the fact that most of my experience has been in the Japanese tradition. Rather than add to a large body of erroneous or misinformed writing on the other arts, I have chosen to keep my comments within an area where my errors will be somewhat more contained.

[5] See the translation by W. Wilson (1979).

[6] The experience of undergoing a *seigan* in Tesshu's *dojo* is recounted in Suzuki (1959:195-197).

[7] For an account of one such historical transmission, see Chan (1963:53).

3. The Ten Oxherding Pictures

Generations of mystics and martial artists have reflected on the pitfalls inherent in the search for enlightenment. They have noted the difficulties involved in pursuing an ascetic discipline, the tendency of the will to falter and the mind to clutter itself with a thousand distractions. The Ten Oxherding Pictures sprung from this tradition. They are at once a blueprint that can outline the process of the search and a message of encouragement that others have trod the same path before. Above all, they are teaching aids that speak to us down the long corridor of years and remind us that we are not alone in our search, our failings, and our potential for ultimate success.

The Ten Pictures are traditionally associated with Master Kuo-an Shih-yuan (Kaku-an Shi-en in Japanese), who practiced Ch'an (Zen) Buddhism during the Sung Dynasty (960-1279) in China. There seems to have been a tradition of using these illustrations as an aid for students—perhaps because their imagery seemed to carry the flavor of Zen experience better than mere text. Through the process of seeking out and taming the ox, the oxherder metaphor illustrates the mental processes involved in the search for enlightenment. While a series of ten illustrations is the best known, other differently-numbered oxherding series preceded this. Seikyo (Ching-chu) probably a Sung-era contemporary, used a series of five pictures to explain Zen. For Seikyo, the ox in the pictures gets gradually whiter until it disappears totally—an obvious metaphor for the attainment of the Zen quality of no-mind (*mu-shin*).

What is interesting from our perspective is that Kaku-an thought Seikyo's five pictures to be misleading, since it makes an empty circle the end point of the enlightenment process. For Master Kaku-an, the end process of Zen enlightenment was the entry of the disciple into the world to spread the benefits of the Zen insight. There was a danger, he seemed to be saying, in making nothingness seem to be the final goal of Zen, and his series of ten pictures was careful to depict the return of the enlightened individual into the sphere of human action. Other commentators seemed to find this opinion compelling, since another series of six pictures reflected the influence of both the five and ten picture series—the ox gets whiter as the disciple approaches enlightenment, but the final illustration shows the oxherder coming back into the world where "every worldly affair is a Buddhist work." (Suzuki 1960:127-8).

In short, these pictures show us that the quest for enlightenment is one that involves both personal spiritual transformation as well as the need to act upon that transformation. Authentic enlightenment goes beyond mere "navel gazing" (or board breaking). It is an event that, in the contradictory way so common to Zen, impels us to both lose a sense of our own self-importance and yet become decisive actors in the social world around us. It is, in short, not just a mystical event, it is a moral one as well.

OXHERDING:

The Ten Stages

The metaphoric process depicting enlightenment is outlined in the Oxherding series as follows:

- Searching for the Ox
- Seeing the Traces
- Seeing the Ox
- Catching the Ox
- Herding the Ox
- Coming Home on the Ox's Back
- The Ox Forgotten, Leaving Man Alone
- The Ox and Man Both Gone Out of Sight
- Returning to the Origin, Back to the Source
- Entering the City With Bliss-Bestowing Hands

From our perspective in the martial arts, we can try to flesh out these episodes by relating them to processes, problems, and perspectives in training. From an organizing perspective, I would like to suggest that we group these ten steps into four broad stages:

I. Searching for a Way

Searching for the Ox

Seeing the Traces

Seeing the Ox

II. Training in the Way

Catching the Ox

Herding the Ox

III. Mastery

Coming Home on the Ox's Back

The Ox Forgotten, Leaving Man Alone

IV. Enlightenment and Moral Action

The Ox and Man Both Gone Out of Sight

Returning to the Origin, Back to the Source

Entering the City With Bliss-Bestowing Hands

I would like to place particular emphasis on the concepts involved in training and moral action, since it seems these are the two areas most commonly neglected in the ways we think about martial arts. On a certain level, the separation of these stages is somewhat misleading. I do not mean to imply that mastery is a destination you arrive at where training is no longer necessary. On the contrary, mastery implies constant, continual training. Nor do I mean to say that moral action is only possible once training is begun or mastery is attained. In fact, these things are all intertwined. For clarity of instruction, however, the Zen masters knew that people needed these different aspects of development broken down so they could better understand them. We would do well to follow their example.

I. Searching for a Way

Searching for the Ox.

At the beginning, the pictures portray a fundamental fact of human existence—confusion. The commentary with the picture describes a man alone in the wilderness, lost in the jungle, with all the sense of isolation and terror that implies. In Buddhist terms, the search is necessary because the oxherd (representing all people) has violated his or her inmost nature and so does not experience reality correctly. The true perception all humans are capable of has been lost. This is represented by the absent ox. The beast is lost and the oxherd has been led out of the way through a variety of delusions brought on by his senses—things like desire and fear.

Seeing the Traces.

Despite this confusion, the Buddhist world-view is an essentially hopeful one. Humans possess the capacity to regain what they have lost. The dissatisfaction of the lost, their intellectual and spiritual hunger for something else, points to a deep-seated need for human beings to return to the path of correct perception and right action. Despite the fact that it is all too easy to succumb to pessimism, to surrender yourself to abandonment, deep down there is something within us that fights this. Mencius, the famous Confucian philosopher, felt that human nature tends toward the good in the same way that water runs downhill. While the human situation may be fraught with complications a bit more complex than gravity, the human dissatisfaction with delusion seems to hint that he was right.

At this stage, the oxherd inquires into doctrines and comes to understand something of what he is seeking. He has found the traces, but his mind is still confused as to what is true and what is not. He has not yet entered the gate. The masters describe this condition with the inscription traditionally associated with this stage: "By the stream and under the trees, scattered are the traces of the lost..."

Seeing the Ox

Through perseverance and honest reflection, the searcher eventually stumbles upon a way that has within it the potential to lead the student to an enhanced type of life. For many of us, this moment comes when we inter into the precincts of a martial arts training hall. We squint into the windows of a storefront *dojo*. Although the sounds escaping are muffled and the figures blurred through the glass, we come to suspect that there is something wondrous going in inside. All that is needed is for us to summon up the courage to enter the door.

This seems a simple thing, but can, in reality, be quite difficult. The world of the *dojo* is, it would seem, a universe apart. It partakes of an older, more measured tradition which creates an environment dramatically at odds with the one most of us are comfortable and familiar with. The study of an art like *karate-do*, for instance, is not only a way to enhanced physical skills. It is also a gateway to a type of culture-shock. It forces you to conform to a different set of parameters and, most importantly from a spiritual viewpoint, to reassess your values and life style.

Just a glance at your surroundings when you enter the precincts of a *karate dojo* sends a message. The training hall, literally the "way place," reflects the austerity and focus of the art itself. There is little in the way of frivolous ornamentation in a traditional *dojo*. The style is functional, and possesses the clean, simple lines of Japanese architecture in general. The *dojo's* design is, in fact, highly reminiscent of the *zendo*, or meditation hall. Very often the only type of ornamentation or design is that present in the *kamiza* or *shomen*, the niche at the head of the room which serves as the "deity seat." It is often marked by a small shrine, some calligraphy, or, with increasing frequency in the modern age, the photograph of a head instructor. These tokens are the symbolic reminders that the *karateka* is a member of a community of students that stretches back through time and across space. The *kamiza* is a visual device that underscores the fact that the training hall is a special place where the student is not merely exercising, but rather participating in an activity which is ultimately concerned with essentially spiritual questions concerning continuity, community, and potential.

When you cross the threshold of a *dojo*, you abandon your outside identity and assume a different one. Your status is not ascribed, but achieved, determined by the propriety of your behavior and the determination and skill you demonstrate in the pursuit of the art. Through the ritual of the bow and the recitation of *dojo kun* (the precepts of the *dojo* normally recited at the end of a training session) you signal your acceptance of the social order of the *dojo* and your willingness to abide by its code.

Karate practitioners, like many other trainees in the modern Japanese martial arts, are ranked in terms of *kyu* and *dan*, and these ranks are symbolized by different colored belts. By looking at the belts worn, it is possible to judge students in terms of their rank and technical proficiency and place them within the *dojo* social hierarchy.

The wearing of a special uniform is also a statement of identity. The white *gi* traditionally worn by *karateka* symbolizes the spiritual nature of training. White is a symbol of death and emptiness in Japanese culture. The conscious adoption of a white training uniform is an attempt to symbolize the trainee's purity, absence of ego and single-minded commitment to the art.

A cursory observation of training in a *karate dojo* reveals that movement is highly regimented and the techniques executed are highly stylized. There is a great deal that is familiar and repetitious in a training session—it is patterned, regular, predictable. There is, in fact, something ritualistic in the flow and direction of training, in the manipulation of symbols and symbolic action.

In overview, we observe the following things. Training is conducted in a special place, the structure of which is designed to send messages concerning the internal significance of the activity. Trainees wear special clothing and have their social relations shaped and colored by their place in a hierarchy unique to the *dojo* itself. They engage in activities charged with impacted meaning—the bows, the recitation of pledges. They are, in fact, engaged in a type of ritual activity.

Like any ritual, participation in training has a number of functions. There is the overt purpose of studying *karate-do* (or any art)—the acquisition of skill. There are also more subtle shadings to the activity. Participation in training is ultimately both a statement of belief and belonging, a tangible signal that the individual holds certain ideals and that he or she holds them in common with a specific community. It is a statement of personal and social identity.

This identity is somewhat different from our "normal selves." As a result, any beginner, of whatever age, finds *karate* difficult, not merely because of the demands it places on physical skill, but because his or her psychic state is at odds with that of the training hall. Once we enter the *dojo* we need to transcend commonplace outlooks and expectations and work to change past habits.

So the challenges faced on entering the threshold of a training hall are many. There is not only the physical challenge of training; there is also tremendous psychic risk there as well. Only an individual focused on transcending personal spiritual limitations will have the fortitude to face such daunting challenges for any length of time. In light of this, a trainee in the martial arts may be engaged in study for quite some time before he or she is capable of seeing the art for what it is and making the full personal commitment needed to fully study it. Thus, the Zen masters speak of the need for the searcher to have his senses in harmonious order as a precondition to actually seeing the ox. Many people can enter into the study of the martial arts; few, however, persevere for long and even fewer continue for the right reasons. Once the trainee breaks through into this state, however, the feeling of arriving is quite dramatic. As the traditional quote that accompanies this stage reads: "The sun is warm and a soothing breeze blows, on the bank the willows are green; The ox is there all by himself, nowhere is he to hide himself..."

II. Training in the Way

Catching the Ox

When we reach this point, the feeling is that we have arrived at some significant threshold. This feeling is authentic, but at the same time that we have arrived we are also launched on a journey. The apprenticeship that each student of a martial art undergoes is long and arduous. In fact, it is a never-ending process. The uninitiated may believe that the purpose of training is to reach the goal of mastery. People familiar with the arts know from experience, however, that such a goal is illusory. We train to better ourselves, it is true, but the standards by which we judge ourselves are themselves transformed over time through the process of training. Anyone who has studied for a time knows that what was considered a skillful performance of technique at the beginner's level becomes something very different as we progress in our training.

This means that new and different challenges will present themselves to us. We will face the frustration of acquiring skills that sometime appear elusive. We will struggle with feelings of inadequacy, or boredom, or even, at more advanced levels, of conceit. Each of these emotions can make the journey a difficult one to traverse.

This is why the Zen masters talk about the challenges of catching the ox. The beast in question is yourself. It is a clumsy brute, sometimes sluggish, sometimes stubborn. The trick is to get the animal harnessed and moving in the right direction. This, the masters knew, is not always easy. They describe a situation where the herder (symbolizing the better part of the self) has at last found the ox and touched him but, due to the pressures of the outside world and its illusions, finds the ox hard to keep under control: "...how wild his will, how ungovernable his power"

Herding the Ox

As always for the Zen masters, the real problem in life centers around the mind and its inability to perceive clearly. Students of the martial arts are very often fixated on questions of a physical nature. This is quite understandable: so much of what we see of the martial arts is expressed in physical terms. To acquire the skills necessary to execute technique is difficult, but it pales in comparison to the difficulty involved in training the mind. It is here, in fact, that the greatest obstacles lie for martial artists.

Let's look at *karate* again. The fact that people train in *karate-do* so assiduously, even in an age where the power of technology in the hands of the untrained has far outstripped the defensive or destructive capabilities of a trained *karateka*, should indicate to us that there is something more going in the precincts of a *karate dojo* than you would expect. Exercise or self-defense are two factors which are often important motivators in getting people to begin the study of *karate-do*, but those who endure in their study almost always find that the art is concerned with much more. The significance of the appendage *do* in *karate-do* indicates that *karate* is a way or path to something, a method that ultimately transcends the rather narrow boundaries of the art itself.

Indeed, I have come to the conclusion that, despite its overtly physical nature, the study of *karate-do* is very much a thing of the mind, a psychological and spiritual journey as well as a physical one. This is the result of both my own experience studying the art and of the insights gained through trying to teach others something of the complexities of this Way.

I began my involvement with the art during college, and I brought to its study all the energy and enthusiasm of a young man. Graduation, work and the later demands of graduate school, marriage and the raising of a family all served to relegate my study of *karate* to the background, however. Although I trained off and on in a variety of martial arts forms and retained my interest in *karate-do* during this intervening period, it was almost ten years before I set foot in a *karate dojo* again. Despite my absence, I was pleasantly surprised at the speed with which I relearned half-forgotten techniques and advanced in skill. It seemed, in fact, that my capacity to learn had improved, not deteriorated, with the passing of years. I found my study of *karate-do* to be even more satisfying and meaningful in middle age than I had as a young man.

I certainly cannot attribute this factor to increased physical ability—the young men and women I trained with were far more flexible and fit than I. Nonetheless, they were the ones who seemed to have a more difficult time of it. Their superior physical condition didn't seem to help them, or at the very least it seemed that physical potential alone was not all that was necessary.

When in time I became skilled enough to help other *karateka* learn the art, I became even more convinced that there seems to be a psychic dimension to the study of *karate* which is in some ways more vital than speed or stamina. I noticed how easily distracted my students were. Three and one-step sparring drills were disjointed exercises, without the seamless flow of attack and response I had come to expect. I noticed in self-defense drills and take-down exercises how the students seemed self-conscious and reluctant to commit fully to the movements required. Worse, they all seemed embarrassed to utter the *kiai*, the shout which punctuates an effective and powerful *karate* technique. In short, they seemed unable to focus totally on the matter at hand—the learning of *karate*.

I thought back to my undergraduate days and remembered the frequency with which my instructors pleaded for more *kime*—more focus—in my techniques. I remembered the constant struggle I waged with even minor problems of balance and movement. I recalled how, no matter how much I said enjoyed studying *karate*, I was always concerned with how much time was left in the lesson. I realize now that what my *sensei* were trying to evoke in me then was not merely the focus needed in any particular technique—a punch with *kime* is noticeably different from one without it—but an overall sense of involvement in and commitment to the task at hand. Focus, they were telling me, not just on the specific technique, but on being fully present in the moment, fully aware, fully engaged. Always a slow student, it took me a decade to catch on.

My pupils, most of whom are college students, have much the same problem I did when I was their age. They are self-conscious. Scattered. Involved in the idea of learning *karate* rather than in the learning itself. They lack a certain ability to focus intently, to commit fully. They too, lack *kime*. More importantly, they have difficulty exhibiting *isshin*—one-heartedness—a cardinal virtue of the *karateka*.

I do not, of course, mean to single young people out. I think the characteristic scattered, self-conscious approach to life, the lack of focus and the corresponding inability to commit fully—with "one heart"—to things is symptomatic of our age and our society. We live in a world obsessed with surface appearance, facile explanations, and quick fixes. It is so fast-paced that it seems nothing else but a surface gloss on life will do. Effort over time, concentration, and attention to details are aspects of life which are considered increasingly irrelevant. Machines do our "drudge work," the video image has replaced the printed page, sound bites have replaced reasoned discourse. We are enmeshed in a whirlwind of rapid sensation, fragmented images, of heat, speed, and noise. In such an environment, we learn to adapt to our surroundings, to prize the ephemeral; it is, after all, the only thing it would seem we can get a hold of.

The world of the martial ways lies in stark contrast to this type of world. It is a place where substance, not appearance, is valued. It seeks to transform, not just entertain people. It, above all, is a challenging place that sends each trainee a message that things worth knowing and doing are rarely easily acquired, that they require hard work, discipline, honesty, and a focus that is frequently absent from our day to day experience.

It is understandable, then, why the mind would wander in such a situation. Many of us are simply not prepared to meet the challenges a martial way places before us. Indeed, a large part of what we do as trainees is learn to surmount these challenges, to develop the inner resources needed to quell our spiritual turmoil.

This is why the Zen masters discussed the process of herding the ox. Through a pursuit of enlightenment, we begin to perceive truth. The restless activity of the mind, however, can continue to distract us and lead to confusion. Strong discipline is necessary to control the self. "Lest," as the masters put it, "the animal should wander away into a world of defilements."

III. Mastery

Coming Home on the Ox's Back

The process of training under the guidance of a skilled instructor can, eventually, lead the trainee safely through the pitfalls of his or her apprenticeship. The process is a long and gradual one, however. We may experience days on the training room floor where that previously elusive technique actually works, where, to speak in terms familiar to the *aikidoka*, the *ki* flows. But we will also be painfully conscious of the slow, almost imperceptible rate at which our training progresses.

This type of dual experience that is commonplace among martial arts trainees—progress that is dramatic contrasted with progress at a snail's pace—has also been noted by adherents of Zen. The Rinzai Zen sect is one that looks for the lightening flash of illumination in the seeker's life, while the Soto Zen sect is one that advocates the role of discipline and application over time in the search for enlightenment. They are, of course, not mutually exclusive. It is possible to struggle for years with the discipline of the spirit, only to have an experience of enlightenment occur with all the unexpected vividness of an explosion.

We have only to look once again at the life of the great Yamaoka Tesshu for such an example.

Tesshu, a Zen priest, studied in the Shinkage Ryu, Ono-ha Itto Ryu and Nakanishi-ha Itto Ryu, becoming one of the premier swordsmen of nineteenth century Japan. What marked Tesshu as a great swordsman, however, was not his physical training, but the emphasis he placed on the disciplining of the mind and spirit. We know that he placed a tremendous emphasis on the role of strict and exhausting training. When he was twenty eight years old, the highly skilled and vibrant Tesshu was decisively defeated by Asari Gimei, master swordsman of the Nakanishi-ha Itto Ryu, a man half Tesshu's size and some twelve years his senior. Asari was such a powerful *kenshi* (swordsman) that Tesshu found himself hopelessly flustered the moment he crossed swords with the master.

Tesshu believed that the solution to this dilemma could be found in training under Asari's tutelage as well as in the rigorous pursuit of enlightenment through the study of Zen. Here he obviously adopted the Soto approach—one emphasizing the cumulative effects of training and discipline. And yet, after seventeen years training in both Asari's and a Zen *dojo*, at age forty five, when Tesshu experienced enlightenment, his experience was an abrupt and transformative one: "For years I forged my spirit through the study of swordsmanship, confronting every challenge steadfastly. The walls surrounding me suddenly crumbled; like pure dew reflecting the world in crystal clarity, total Awakening has now come."

The lesson for martial artists seems to be one in which they are enjoined to work diligently at their training and yet cautioned that enlightenment—when and if it comes—is rarely what is expected.

In fact, it may be that Tesshu's experience shows us that the virtue of training is not that it "leads" us anywhere, but that it eventually helps us forget our obsessions with "getting" anywhere in the first place. In this way the novice's hunger for a black belt should evaporate by the time he or she attains that rank. It has, it is hoped, become meaningless on a certain level. Here again, the idea that the ways in which we measure our progress change along with the progress we make comes into play. That fact that a *yudansha* can execute a *kata—nage no kata* in *judo*, or *kanku-dai* in *karate-do*, for instance—with a measure of skill that is beyond the novice's level is meaningless for that advanced student. What is of concern is how the *budoka* meets the challenge of the particular *kata* for him or herself in the here and now, at the current level of skill. This has the effect of doing away with a goal-oriented mind-set. The task at hand has been transformed to performing the *kata*, not at a particular skill level, but as well as possible. In this way, we work at perfecting our skill while at the same time abandoning any expectation of ever arriving at the illusory end-point of "perfection." Here, in a type of alert forgetfulness, we enter the next stage

The Ox Forgotten, Leaving Man Alone

When we have abandoned the self-consciousness of the novice and give ourselves over totally to the art, when we surrender any notion that we can ever possibly perfect our techniques (although we will continue to try), then we have reached a state where, in forgetting ourselves and any goals we may have had, we attain a type of unity with the art we study. In the state where there is a total merging of martial art and martial artist, the quality of *mushin* is found.

At this point, the ox we have worked so long and hard to tame is revealed as another type of illusion. While the petty distractions and concerns of life that have cluttered up our mind are easily recognized to be obstacles in our search, eventually even the mind itself is revealed as a more subtle form of impediment.

When we have mastered the control of this ox, we are able to abandon all concern and even awareness of it. Thus, the masters tell us, at this juncture, "the ox is no more." In the state of *mu-shin* the individual demonstrating this quality has a clear mind, endowed with an enhanced type of perception. The Zen illustration of no-mind *(mushin-no-shin)* is that of a placid pool of water that perfectly reflects the moon.

The notion of a type of awareness that permits an individual to immediately react to something was, and continues to be, extremely attractive to martial artists. The "stopping" effect of the mind, its ability to distract us at critical junctures, to be so engrossed in expecting one thing that a surprising technique isn't anticipated, is an experience common to many trainees. When the Zen masters talked about the aspect of no-mind, it was clear to Japan's *samurai* warriors that a mind as calm and unruffled as a pool facilitates the ability of the martial arts master.

This is a point that Japan's feudal swordsmen sought in both their training and in the integration of Zen precepts in their studies. The famous swordsman Yagyu Munenori was a student of the noted Zen master Takuan Soho, who used illustrations from the art of swordsmanship to discuss the workings of the mind and the effect of enlightenment. He taught: "You must follow the movement of the sword in the hands of the enemy, leaving your mind free to make its own counter-movement without interfering deliberation. You move as the opponent moves, and it will result in his own defeat." Here was a graphic illustration of *mu-shin* that suggests to us how the state of mastery is expressed in the physical language of the *dojo*.

IV. Enlightenment and Moral Action

The critical point in the pursuit in any martial way, however, is not the worship of prowess and technical accomplishment. In other words, it is not what you can do in the martial arts, it is what you can do *with* the martial arts. It is a subtle distinction, made more obscure by the sad fact that so many people seem uninterested in following its implications out, but, as I have indicated, it is the most important redeeming dimension to martial arts practice.

For if we, as martial artists, are merely concerned with the development of technical skills and their role in self-aggrandizement, we have sadly missed the mark. That type of focus makes training in the martial ways a pointless and foolish activity: human beings lavishing time and effort on the mastery of archaic weapons systems that are wholly inadequate to the challenge of violence in the modern world. It would be a sterile activity, bled of any relevance and incapable of lending any guidance on the pressing question of being fully human.

Of course, the whole point of the martial arts as I understand them is to transcend the narrow realm of violence and assist trainees to somehow elevate themselves, to rise above the heat and confusion and fear of life, and find something profound and worthwhile. My colleague David Jones, an advanced *aikidoka* and gifted scholar, suggests that there is a type of alchemy going on in the martial arts: that, despite their undeniable links to violence and pain, it is possible to distill something noble in the human spirit through their practice.

A quality much prized by martial artists is that known as *zanshin*. The word literally translates as "remaining mind." We can gloss it as "awareness." In *kendo*, for instance, it is critical to exhibit good *zanshin* before, during, and (most significantly) after the execution of technique. The awareness demonstrated by the swordsman must be of such a caliber that he or she is always ready to attack or respond to attack and is highly sensitized to the surroundings. By insisting on the display of *zanshin* even after a technique, *kendo sensei* are setting very high standards for their pupils. What they are seeking, in effect, is a sign that students cannot be distracted by fear (if their stroke fails) or elation (if they score a point) or anything else. The *kendo* masters are looking for a demonstration of a type of awareness, focus and (in that maddeningly Zen-like way of being contradictory) transcendence. They want to see whether the student has reached a point where, for however fleeting a moment, he or she can be totally enmeshed in *kendo*, undistracted by the conscious thought of "I am doing *kendo*" or "I am doing *kendo* well" or "I am doing *kendo* badly." They want to see if the student has developed a different, more heightened, sense of awareness that transcends concerns focused exclusively on the self.

In fact, when you extend the notion of *zanshin* to another plane entirely, you are beginning to talk about a quality that, although it seems to be about an intense kind of focus on the here and now, is really about losing all concern with yourself and redirecting your focus onto the rest of the world.

I believe that the most profound expression of *zanshin* is an enhanced awareness of our links with one another and a strengthened commitment to communal action where the balance, poise and wisdom achieved in the *dojo* can contribute toward the ways in which we act in the social world.

The Ox and Man Both Gone Out of Sight

In other words, the courage we learn in the *dojo* requires that we be courageous in other spheres as well. I am not talking about comic book heroics, but a type of quiet, patient, firm, and forgiving courage that is much harder to maintain in real life. To do so requires a truly enhanced vision of what is important and essential as well as the spirit and tenacity to follow that vision, no matter how difficult.

To do this requires, at least partially, a significant surrender of the notion of self. We know that, as social animals, human beings are extremely sensitive to the opinions of others. Peer pressure, "face," public opinion have the power to sway us away from our goals. In many ways, the impact of others' opinion is so strong because so much of our identity is a social construction, dependent on those around us for life.

And yet we know that we are more than just the sum of others' opinions. Certainly the world's great religious traditions point to a reality that transcends any particular social setting and serves to guide us in truly authentic behavior. If we can attain a grasp of that reality, and focus on that (as opposed to ourselves) we stand a far better chance of living a fully human life.

Zen is part of this tradition. When we attain enlightenment, the Zen masters tell us, confusion is set aside; serenity prevails. "Manifest is the spirit of the ancient master."

The Sanskrit term for enlightenment, *satori*, literally refers to a blowing out, like the action of blowing out the flame on a candle. The image is a striking one, particularly for Westerners, since the primacy of the individual, our search for distinctiveness, and a long tradition that seeks (despite notable and horrific actions to the contrary) to celebrate the dignity of the human person is strongly entrenched in our minds. In the Buddhist tradition, however, this holding on to the individual self can pose a problem in that it interferes with our ability to relate truly and directly with experience. If nothing else, Zen attempts to bring its adherents into more direct contact with life, and to wear away the individual shell that distorts our grasp of true reality.

In the martial arts, as we have seen, this individual shell can pose an obstacle. Once it has been surmounted, we have the experience of a more direct, immediate link with the essential nature of things. At this juncture, considerations of the self, and even of the art, become immaterial.

We are, in fact, progressing towards a point that Buddhists feel is closer to our true nature (since it is the same as the true nature of the universe). This is expressed through the next picture:

Returning to the Origin, Back to the Source

At this juncture, the martial artist enters a realm many of us (the author included) can only aspire to: authentic experience of such a nature that it is virtually impossible to describe. This acknowledgment is one of the constant themes of all written works regarding mysticism (and the Zen experience fits very well in this category): words are inadequate to explain the phenomenon. In the classic imagery used by the Zen masters, all our descriptions and directions are like the finger pointing at the moon: they are meant to somehow direct us to what we seek, yet should never be confused with the goal itself.

This inability being duly acknowledged, what we can discuss is the fact that the potential for attaining this state exists. It is a condition that must be analogous to the experience of almost continual "flow." Things are seen more clearly, life experienced more immediately. We feel so connected to things that questions of "control" are meaningless, if only because the distinction between controller and controlled has been negated. At this point, we have arrived at the exhilarating and terrifying peak of experience, at the end of a long road along which the trainee began travelling so long ago.

Entering the City With Bliss-Bestowing Hands

But perhaps the most important stage from my perspective is the last one. For, in reality, we have not reached the end of our journey. We have in fact, embarked on a new and more significant one. For what happens when an individual reaches the juncture where questions of self and other are negated, where a true perception of reality is achieved? On achieving this state do we lapse into quiescence, content with the stereotypical "navel gazing" detractors speak about when they critique Asian philosophical systems?

The Oxherding Pictures would seem to indicate otherwise. The enlightened being does not remain unconnected from the world and its peoples like some spiritual miser unwilling to share his or her wealth. On the contrary, the Oxherding Pictures are emphatic in pointing out that reaching such a state is not the end of the journey. What is required next is not a total flight from the world, but a total immersion in it.

By returning, the individual brings the opportunity for others to experience the same spiritual development. The Buddhist text indicates that, by entering into the realm of human affairs, such an individual converts all into Buddhas: "There is no need for the miraculous powers of the gods, For he touches, and lo! the dead trees are in full bloom."

For our purpose, the significance of this insight is in the way it highlights the absolutely necessary connection of the martial artist with wider society. The search for skill, perfection, enlightenment—whatever various seekers name it—is ultimately a sterile pursuit unless its effects somehow spill over into the wider web of social connections that each individual maintains.

The experience of past masters can once again aid us in understanding this dimension of martial arts training. As Yagyu Munenori struggled with the questions each serious martial artist must eventually face, he found the guidance he needed through Zen and his long association with the monk Takuan. It would have been easy for Munenori to settle into a complacent type of surface "mastery." His technique was peerless, his social standing as the Shogun's fencing instructor was secure. He had achieved many of the outward trappings of success. But Munenori was a tenacious student, and his progress led him to believe that there was something more to his studies.

Partially due to Takuan's guidance, Munenori came to believe that righteousness is an essential part of the martial arts. Without this moral dimension, swordsmanship became merely the act of killing and avoiding being killed. Demonstrating the impact of Zen on his outlook, Munenori believed that swordsmen must aspire to cast off petty distractions if they are to achieve real mastery. And, most importantly, he believed that once in this state it was incumbent on the individual to act for the good of others.

Munenori was convinced that his swordsmanship could and should make a positive contribution to society. I will maintain that this concept is implicit in all fully mature martial arts (and martial artists). Munenori was one in a long tradition of swordsmen convinced that the proper study of martial arts led to a spiritual insight and moral maturity which could not fail to have a beneficial impact on society.

If summation, we can see that Munenori's most enduring contribution to the practice of the Japanese martial arts is not just his stress on Zen concepts as a route to mastery, but his insistence that true swordsmanship is a moral art. "*Katsujinken Satsujinken*" is a motto hung on the *dojo* of the Yagyu Shinkage Ryu, and is also found on teaching licences awarded to advanced students. Literally "the sword that gives life, the sword that takes life" this phrase is an enduring reminder of the real nature and responsibility of training in the martial ways.

This sensibility is encapsulated in the modern martial ways today. Like many subtle things, however, it is quite possible to overlook it. The sheer physicality of the arts—their dynamism, force, and apparent ferocity—often act to obscure a more complex understanding. Yet, at advanced levels of training, the practitioner comes to appreciate just how empty skill is unless the student has internalized many of the lessons learned along the path of training. Strength wanes. Speed fades. Ultimately, what matters in the pursuit of the martial arts is not the level of our accomplishment within them, but how we use our experiences to illuminate the struggles we all face on a day to day level. Most importantly, what is of central concern is the development of an awareness of our obligation to others. Without the conviction that we should act for the good in society, and without the will to carry such actions out, our pursuit of the martial way runs the risk of deteriorating into a self-centered exercise in futility

True mastery, in other words, is a call to *zanshin*, the ability to forget ourselves, focus completely on others, and act according to the highest precepts embodied in the martial ways. Only then will we have achieved the authentic life that the Oxherding Pictures hint at.

4. The Oxherder's Journal

I am drawn to the *dojo* again and again. I gaze through the steamy glass of storefront schools with the same wide-eyed wonder and desire of a child ogling a toy display at Christmas. In fact, what began for me as an essentially intellectual enterprise—the academic study of a particular aspect of Japanese culture—has changed into something more. The almost magnetic pull of the modern martial arts is, I believe, an attraction which far transcends their ostensible value as either exercise or systems of self defense. I am not alone in this feeling or in this suspicion, for while there are literally millions of martial arts practitioners in the world, only a tiny fragment ever attain the proficiency of champions or exhibit the psychological predisposition of the natural fighter. For the most part, *budoka* labor at their training—and anyone who studies *budo* will tell you that it is mostly hard work—

without the ruthless determination of the competitor or the grim focus of the warrior. Elements of fear, aggression, and competition are present, of course, but they are not the sole motivation for study. Martial artists, I have come to believe, are engaged in something that is complex, significant, and fully human—something that transcends the narrow (though important) bounds of the arena and spills over into life in its fullest sense.

Martial arts are popularly understood simply as methods of fighting that are weaponless or utilize the archaic arsenal of a foreign culture's bygone age. When people think of the martial arts they envision the seemingly effortless grace of judo flips or the destructive impact of the karate chop. Certainly the promise of heightened defensive and offensive powers is part of the attraction the martial arts hold for people today—witness the seemingly endless series of martial arts movies. Anyone who perseveres in their study of these arts, however, must certainly be seeking something more. The "something more" they find is as multidimensional as the arts themselves and as varied as the individuals who study them. Some indication of the broad dimensions of meaning people find in *dojo* can be gleaned simply from the way martial artists talk about what they do.

As we have mentioned, *budoka* describe their activities in many different ways, and these descriptions convey something of the wide spectrum of functions the martial arts assume for people. Individuals may "study" an art—a word that reveals the intellectual predispositions of the Western mind as well as the sentiment that the martial arts are something worthy of serious (which to the West means intellectual) consideration. Other *budoka* "play," a usage that reflects, I suspect, the translation of the Japanese word concerning activities surrounding things as varied as cooking, using mystical instruments, and engaging in sports. *Judoka*, for instance, always sat that they are playing judo. This reflects judo's strong sport identity in the modern world (it has been an Olympic event since 1964). I also think it has a deeper significance: its use is an implicit recognition of one of the central tenets of the art—the expression of *ju*, or gentleness, through the pursuit of mutual benefit and welfare. The use of "play" is a tacit acknowledgment by judo students that very few of them will ever attain the skills or statuses of champions. They play, in short, for sheer enjoyment of the beauty of the art.

A final often-heard description is that of "training." This can reflect as variety of orientations. Competitors train. The use of the this word conveys a seriousness of purpose which is found among *budoka* who are contest oriented, or whose particular style is heavily concerned with self-defense and combat. This is a particularly grim approach, and one in which the true meaning of *budo* can be obscured if great care is not taken. To focus only on contest is to be fixated on winning and losing, to define oneself solely on the basis of a fleeting moment. It is, of course, a highly human sort of thing to do, since we are by nature goal oriented, but there is little of a martial "way" in this sort of study. In the relentless pursuit of victory we run the risk of not preparing for the inevitable event in human life—defeat. We make the art a means to an end (and a very limited end a that), rather than a thing to be savored and enjoyed for its own sake.

This is not to say that the pursuit of the martial arts is not a serious thing, for it most certainly is. Nor do I mean to say that competition has no place in *budo*. I merely caution aspiring martial artists (as I must constantly caution myself) to be fully aware of the nature of the activity being engaged in and not to lose either perspective or the capacity for self-criticism. As a mater of fact, most traditionally-oriented martial arts will always refer to martial arts activity as training. The traditional use of the term, however, implies a much more comprehensive meaning than the one used above. This has important implications for our emphasis on the spiritual dimension of the martial arts.

Training encompasses study, in the sense that we reflect lessons passed on to us from our teachers. The study of *budo* is a gateway into Japanese history and society. It is a cultural activity in the broadest sense—we learn of the thoughts, insights, and lessons of past masters and apply them to our lives today. *Budo* is not just an intellectual enterprise, however. We are also engaged in a type of physical activity which is often conditioned by specific rules and methods of execution tacitly accepted by other trainees to obtain a variety of physical and psychological benefits. A ritualized, rule-bound type of activity which offers enjoyment on a number of levels is of course, a type of sport, and sports are played.

Ultimately, we are doing all these things, and something more. We are, as a *kendo sensei* told me, training, not for contest, not for promotion, but for life. The lessons learned on the hard wood floor or the padded surface of the *dojo,* are ones that transcend technique, that go beyond categorizations of people into groups of winners and losers. These lessons are about fine-tuning the body, clearing the mind; about uniting these two often warring aspects of the person in such a way as to combat the sense of fragmentation and purposelessness so common in society today. They are about joining together with other people in an often intense and violent activity which in the end brings people together, not drives them apart. And, finally, these lessons are about exploring the boundaries and possibilities of being fully human.

One of the ways in which the student's imagination is engaged in the process of learning something about the more complex aspect of martial ways is through the apocryphal stories told regarding masters of the arts. These stories may or may not be true in the historical sense. On a certain level, their veracity is not even important. What matters is that these stories are told and retold by martial artists and are believed to hold some sort of significance and impart some sort of lesson. In a sense they are the myths of the martial arts world—significant tales that are passed on by generations of believers. Very often the lessons contained in such "martial myths" are complex ones: they reveal themselves gradually over time and one's understanding of them evolves with the progress made in the arts themselves.

In light of the emphasis on moral action I am advocating, I would like to examine some myths and subject them to an interpretation that is somewhat unique. I should caution the reader that my interpretation is not the only way these myths can be understood; it is rather an exploration of one facet of the very complex phenomenon of the martial ways.

ISSHIN

In the recesses of an abandoned granary the strong light of the countryside was swallowed up in shadow. It was cool in there, a coldness like newly turned earth before the Spring gets to work on it. Maybe it was the dark or the dampness or the frigid feeling like something ancient and waiting, but the murderer fled there like someone heading home.

The boy was terrified of course. He had been gathering small sticks and bits of straw for his mother's fire, wandering along the lesser used paths outside the village. Sound caries far in the country, and he had sensed the thudding of feet long before the man shot into view around a bend. The thing was done in an instant, the boy pinned and dragged along with the fleeing man. He was dense and large and dirty. The battered hilt of a short sword was stuck in his sash. His breath came in great gulps as he stumbled down the path, shooting hurried glances over his shoulder. He had thick, strong fingers with dirty, broken nails. They grasped the boy cruelly, and when the boy cried out, the man cuffed him with a quick harshness that shocked the child into silence.

In the intuitive way children have, the boy knew he was in the presence of evil.

The pursuers ran them to ground in the granary. There was a crowd of farmers, the potter, the local blacksmith—men who knew all the local ways someone could try to escape. They all knew the boy, too. Once the murderer and his hostage disappeared into the building the crowd paused, momentarily at a loss.

"Anyone comes any closer, I'll cut his throat." It was a raspy, matter of fact voice. The man edged a bit nearer the doorway, his blade held across the boy's neck. Everyone in the crowd had been raised in the country. They had seen how easy it was to slit an animal's throat many times—seen how fragile life's container was. None of them had any doubt that the man would do what he said. None of them thought there was any way to prevent him.

"We should send for the constable," the potter whispered.

"Idiot," the blacksmith countered." It'll take hours. By that time, he'll be long gone. And once he's gone. . ." he drew a finger across his throat, "He doesn't need the boy."

The discussion dissolved into futile suggestions, sounds of despair. A crowd gathered, intent that the murderer should not escape, but intent on saving the boy, and equally perplexed about how to go about doing it.

A small group of men came into view down the road. They had obviously been traveling: their sandals were dirty and their robes had been hitched up to avoid the mud. The crowd slowly grew silent as they approached, eyeing each other warily: these were *samurai*. Their clothes, their distinctive top-knot hairstyle, but most of all, the *daisho*—the short and long sword of the warrior—they each carried gave them a fierce, predatory look.

The crowd sank to the ground and bowed deeply, a new element of anxiety adding to their consternation. *Samurai* were notoriously unpredictable. In the hierarchy of things, farmers were said to be the backbone of the country, but the real power lay in the hands of the men with swords. Warriors ate the rice the farmers grew, but often treated them like the dirt they spent their lives working.

The oldest man present approached the swordsmen and, with a great deal of bowing and apologies, explained the situation. The swordsmen began to murmur, loosening their blades and spreading out for action. They seemed excited by the prospect of fighting, the chance to bring a murderer to justice, and the potential it all had for their reputations as warriors. The villagers grew more agitated. Could it be possible that the *samurai* failed to see the real problem? It wasn't that they had a murderer trapped here; it was that a boy from their village was being held hostage.

The village elder began to stammer, trying to figure out a way to stop what seemed like an inevitable blood bath.

"Wait." The oldest swordsman was smaller than the others. He had an impassive face with deep lines cut by seasons of squinting in the sun of countless battlefields. Compared to his burlier companions he seamed almost frail, although he had the thick, over-developed forearms of a swordsman. The others deferred to him, however.

For the first time, the village elder spoke directly to the leader, bypassing the conventional go-between. It was a risk, since the swordsman could take great offense, but what was he to do? Remain silent and have to explain to the boy's parents that, yes the boy died, but the social niceties were never violated?

The swordsman listened again to the elder's explanation, standing there quietly, not interrupting, and asking only a few questions when the elder was done. How was the man armed? How long had he been fleeing? How big was the boy?

The *bushi* sighed to himself, rubbing his chin as he tried to think of a way to solve the problem. A frontal assault was out—while there was no question his disciples would cut the man down, the boy would most certainly die as well.

He sighed again. Such a waste of life. He had seen a great deal of blood spilled in his time. In a way, he had spent his life studying the most efficient ways of doing just that, traveling with his disciples across the country, looking to perfect his skills. But he hated to see innocent life lost and, in a strange way, felt that saving the occasional innocent might somehow make up for the long roll of men he had dispatched.

The problem here was that he could see no way of saving the boy. So he squatted down and waited.

His students hated this about him. They were young and full of energy. They itched to use their skills. The master constantly reminded them, however, that waiting was a skill as well. So they all waited, the warriors and the people in the crowd, while the sun crept across the sky and the shadows began to lengthen.

"Hey out there. I want water. Food. Bring it to me." From the shadows the boy squealed briefly in pain as the murderer punctuated his demands.

The villagers looked at the master for guidance. They were all a bit afraid to approach the granary—after all, there was no reason to make things worse or tempt fate. At the same time, if one of the hot-blooded young swordsmen were picked, there was no telling what might happen.

The master stood up, stretching his back. "Ahh. . ."

"I will go," came a voice from the crowd. A monk, drawn to the commotion, had been sitting there for some time. The master looked at the monk as if seeing him for the first time—the shaved head and saffron robe of office symbols of this man's total devotion to compassion and his complete removal from the concerns of the world. The perfect emissary.

It took some time to assemble the food and water—more time than you would think to find a water gourd and some rice balls. The boy's whimpering could sometimes be heard by the crowd. Eventually the monk emerged and slowly approached the granary. He walked a bit unsteadily, as if afraid to do what he was sent to do. He wobbled along the weedy path to the door, eventually ending up on its right hand side. The murderer had eyed his approach with contempt but moved cautiously into the middle of the door to keep an eye on the monk.

"That's far enough." The monk was unarmed, but a lifetime of caution told the murderer to keep him at least an arm's length away. He still held on to the boy with one hand and his sword with the other.

"I am unarmed," the monk said. Despite his wobbly approach his voice seamed calm and quiet. But who could feel threatened by a monk? "Here is food," he said, holding out two rice balls. The murderer began to reach out, hunger driving away some caution. "Here. I will come no nearer." The monk gently tossed the ball of rice. The man relaxed his grip on the short sword—it was attached to his wrist by a cord—and caught the ball. Without pause, the monk tossed the other one in the same gentle manner.

The murderer fumbled for a split second to manage the boy, the rice ball he held, and the one tossed to him. In a flash, the man the killer thought was a monk was on him. A crashing blow, a twist of the arm, and the killer's feet were swept out from under him.

"Tie him up," the master said to his disciples as they rushed the granary. Then, walking back down the path to the crowd, he said, "Thank you for the loan of your garment, monk. Whatever you may believe, for today at least there is a little less suffering in the world."

The master walked through the crowd, ruefully rubbing his newly shaven head and wondering how long it would take to grow a top-knot back.

As human beings, the world of the senses offers us great joy and great danger. Buddhists speak of the problem of *maya* (illusion) as an impediment to enlightenment. It is not only that the senses can deceive us; the problem is often that we set too great a store by appearances.

The vignette I have presented above is a famous one in the martial arts—it was even used by Akira Kurasowa as the opening scene of *The Seven Samurai*. The way it is generally interpreted is as a demonstration of how the incredible skill of a martial artist can be put to use righting wrongs or helping the innocent. In a sense, this is true. I think it is even more importantly an exploration of how the martial artist's obligation to society—for with great skill comes great responsibility—can impel him or her to transcend a concern with appearances and illusions.

Notice in the story that the essential trick that is being played on the murderer is one that surrounds perception. In this case, the master swordsman disguises himself as a Buddhist monk—a peaceful, unthreatening, somewhat inept person—to effect the boy's rescue. The outer badges of a monk's identity—a shaven head, a distinctive type of clothing—delude the killer into permitting the master to get within range. The murderer is by definition deluded, since his mind has been clouded by rage, and the master knows this and uses it against him.

The importance of symbolic trappings in this story has something else to tell us, however. We have to remember that the country where this story took place, feudal Japan, was a deeply class-conscious one. Like many societies of this type, class distinctions were expressed in terms of dress, hairstyle, manners, and even language. Even today, it is possible to listen to two Japanese people speaking and guess, merely from the level of polite language each uses, which speaker has a higher social status.

In feudal Japan, members of the warrior, farmer, and merchant classes were easily identified. They dressed differently (a variety of sumptuary laws even specified what type of fabrics non-*samurai* were allowed to wear). Their hairstyles were distinct, as well. The men of the warrior class had the top of their heads shaved and grew a top-knot that was combed forward. At around age five, *samurai* boys were symbolically initiated into their warrior status in a ceremony where they stood on a *go* board (symbolizing strategy) and presented with a toy sword. Their heads were also shaved in the manner described above. So from a very early age, warriors were aware of how the way they looked was related to who they really were.

The fact that Buddhist monks shaved their heads was a real symbol of their renunciation of the world and its social order. *Samurai* sometimes entered the monkhood, but usually when they were old men and their utility as warriors was done. In any other situation, to lose your top-knot was a source of real humiliation.

But here we are presented with a story where a master swordsman—a man whose entire life was devoted to refining the arts that helped define the *samurai* as a class—voluntarily shaves his head to do a good deed. It may not seem terribly significant to readers today, but this was an unheard of thing. This was a society where the warrior class took for granted their superiority and viewed all other people as essentially existing to service the needs of the upper class. This kind of world view breeds a certain callousness. In fact, any *samurai*, anywhere, who felt that they had even been insulted by a lower-class person, had the legal right to kill that person on the spot and walk away, no questions asked. The gulf between warriors and others was that wide.

The lesson, although centuries old, is relevant for martial artists today. You only have to observe the many subtle ways in which rank and status are indicated in *dojo* to understand that questions of pride and humility are enduring ones, and that even today we create illusory chasms between ourselves and others. The hunger for rank and advancement on the part of novices is a common phenomenon in many training halls. The white belt stumbles onto the floor, gazing with envious eyes at the *yudansha*. They wear *hakama*. Or *obi*, somber, dark as night, heavy with mystery. They are, to the uninitiated, the embodiment of skill and arcane knowledge that is part of the allure of the arts. They are different, more experienced, more skilled. It is quite common for all involved to believe that they are somehow superior.

Here the danger of illusion is as real for the trainee as it was for the murderer in the story. In the environment of the training hall, it is easy for the more advanced student to let things get to his or her head. It is easy to forget that the trainee is always, in some ways, a novice, and needs to approach training (and relations with others) with that in mind. Many of us can remember coming across individuals who, although skilled, were tremendously self-satisfied about the fact (as if all skill is not relative); seniors who were more interested in impressing others with their competence than with helping their juniors gain some insight into the art.

In *judo dojo*, for instance, a central concern for all lower ranks (whether they admit it or not) is to try to identify which *yudansha* will help beginners to learn and which will merely use *randori* as a way to pound home the fact that a black belt can make a lower rank fall down in a number of different ways. In good *dojo*, the *sensei* usually monitors this situation and is not averse to stepping in to teach the senior student a little humility. This is, in fact, an important lesson that needs to be imparted. After working so long and so hard to gain a certain level of skill, students indulge in the quite understandable feeling that they have accomplished something admirable. They have, of course, but they are not done learning. Above all, they run the risk of thinking about themselves more than they think about the art. In such a situation, they lose the focus and seriousness that the martial arts demand. By celebrating their own accomplishments, by forgetting the more complex goals of training , and, above all, by forgetting their obligation to others, they lose the quality of single-heartedness, or *isshin*, that is so important in martial arts training. They are not a violent type of criminal like the man in the story, but the same flaw that makes them arrogant causes them to lose their capacity to become actors in a positive moral sense in the human community

The swordsman in the story is obviously someone who has transcended the conceit that comes with accomplishment. He is devoted to his art, not to himself. His sincere pursuit of the way, despite the discomfort and danger it brings him, is an example of the quality of *isshin*. This man was a master swordsman. His skill was so great that he had attracted a body of students who followed him around. His confidence was so strong that he traveled the country seeking out opponents to vanquish. He may have traveled through the countryside, but in social terms he barely touched the ground as far as local farmers were concerned. Yet he pauses in his journey and voluntarily submits to a type of humiliation in order to save the life of a total stranger—and a lower class stranger at that—when it would have been a great deal more convenient to let the local authorities try to solve what was really a parochial and rather squalid situation that could do little for his reputation as a fighter.

Why?

I believe that this is the crux of the story. Disarming an armed man is an impressive feat. The power of the art in subduing a madman pales, however, next to the force it exerts on the master. For by virtue of his pursuit of the way, he is compelled to transcend the limitations of his own pride and concern for public opinion, and to do what is right. His sincere pursuit of the way, despite the discomfort and danger it brings him, is an example of the quality of *isshin*—single heartedness—that is a central part of training in a martial way, and of the moral dimension implicit in walking this path.

MUSHIN

Late at night, he burned.

Katsuyoshi was a proud man, and even in sleep he could not flee from shame. He would train, grunting and straining through the humid days, his staff sweeping in flashing arcs, reversing, thrusting, until his surroundings dimmed in the gray-blue onset of twilight and his shoulders were cooled with the falling of dew. Then he would sit, calming his breathing, his heart slowly thudding into a slower tempo.

He would review the lessons of the day in the tidal wash of pulse and breath. He felt the tension in his legs and arms burn away. In time, the night whirring of insects grew and grew in volume, magnified as the light died, and drove conscious thought from his mind. Sometimes, as he felt himself drifting away, it was almost as if the match had never taken place. He felt something almost like the peace of former years.

Then he would close his eyes and, in a horrible flash, relive the moment—the stutter in his step, the flawed attack. His opponent's wooden swords trapped his staff. He was checked, thrown off balance and, in a flash, was confronted with the blurring slash of the *bokken* that ended a hair's breadth from his neck. Defeat.

It was an experience no less bitter in his dreams.

Gonosuke Katsuyoshi had driven himself from a very young age to master the arts of the warrior. As a child, he had been beaten and humiliated by older boys. It was an incident whose cause even Katsuyoshi had forgotten—like many things of childhood, the precise details seemed to fade with the passing years. What never left him, though, was the shame he felt as he lay, bruised and beaten, in the dirt of the crossroads, nor the resolve he had limped home with: to someday be a warrior that all men feared.

He grew into a prideful young man who, despite his unimpressive physical presence, had an uncanny gift for the art of the sword. With a weapon in his hand, he seemed to swell, growing more confident and menacing in appearance. He trained with a devotion and barely contained ferocity that was fueled, even as an adult, by the emotions of hurt and shame and fear he had experienced so very vividly as a child.

He mastered the techniques and strategy of the Tenshin Shoden Katori Shinto Ryu. Then the Kashima Ryu. He wielded the *katana*, the *naginata*, and the *yari*, coming to know their qualities and uses with an almost instinctual transference that seemed to occur merely by holding the weapons in his hand.

But his teachers, while impressed by his skill, remained unsatisfied with other areas of his development. Sitting together sipping tea, they appeared stolid and unperceptive: thick men in well-worn *keikogi*. Their eyes told a different story, however. They glittered with alertness and could fix a trainee with a piercing glance. They appreciated Katsuyoshi's achievements, but saw them as somehow incomplete. They challenged him to explore other arts, other weapons, in the hopes that a new perspective or new frustrations would generate something within him that mere technical mastery seemed not to have done. Eventually, despairing of their prodigy, his masters had encouraged him to become a *mushashugyosha*, an itinerant warrior who wandered the land in search of new venues in which to conquer (or be conquered). Some day, the group of *sensei* hoped, Katsuyoshi would discover that even his immense talent could be defeated, and that this experience would temper his spirit and introduce him to the critical element currently lacking in his mastery: humility.

He had wandered throughout the seemingly endless chain of hills, threading different forest roads to the bright clearings of towns. He churned the length of central Japan, seeking out new masters and *dojo* to test his skills. He grew so proud that he once more picked up the staff, that most simple of weapons, so confident in his skill that he would face a swordsman with nothing but a shaft of *kashiwa* oak. He left a trail of opponents in his wake, and each humbled challenger lying panting on the ground helped ease the memory of a little boy lying bleeding in a dusty road two decades ago.

Then he met Musashi.

He was a scruffy looking character, ill-kempt and slightly bug-eyed. He walked, however, with a swagger that seemed somehow familiar to Katsuyoshi—and any observer with the nerve could have told him that was because both these warriors had the same look of defiant arrogance. Once they had been introduced, it was inevitable that a match would be arranged.

It was held early one morning in a clearing by a narrow river. Tendrils of mist still steamed up from the water's surface as Katsuyoshi waited for his opponent to appear. They had agreed on dawn for the match, but here in the narrow mountain valley the sky had lightened long before the sun peered over the eastern rim of hills. Katsuyoshi wondered whether Musashi had forgotten; even allowing for a misunderstanding of what dawn meant, surely he would want to examine the field? Many a warrior had been defeated by things other than technique, and the secret transmissions of many sword *ryu* dealt with admonitions to examine your surroundings carefully, and to use these things—the slope of the land, the angle of the sun—in your strategy.

Musashi came boiling into the clearing and, without any but the most minimal preliminaries, tied up his sleeves, handed his swords to a companion, and drew a pair of wooden swords from a bag.

"*Bokken?*" Katsuyoshi asked.

Musashi nodded nonchalantly and shrugged at the staff his opponent held. "Your wood against mine."

Katsuyoshi regretted the choice. Sometimes, just the confidence he displayed by daring to go against a live blade with an oak staff was enough to shake an opponent. Besides, carefully used, it was possible for a wooden *bo* to actually shatter the steel of a *katana.* It was hard to tell whether Musashi's choice was a reflection of his confidence, his cunning, or even both. Katsuyoshi felt a small thrill of anticipation: this would be an interesting match.

And so it was. There were few spectators, and those that were present were silent. Except for the murmur of the river and the distant chirping of birds, the only sounds that could be heard were the swish of the swordsmen's *hakama*, the rush of their breath, and the sharp clacking of their weapons as each man furiously sought the critical opening that would decide the encounter.

It was not totally unheard of for a swordsman to use two swords at once, but Katsuyoshi was startled with the skill Musashi displayed, wielding them, now in tandem, now in separate movements, so that his opponent was continually on guard. It became gradually apparent to both men that the flow and celerity of technique being displayed that day was of a higher order. The few senior *kenshi* watched with narrowed, appreciative eyes.

Some of the apprehension Katsuyoshi felt early in the match began to fade, however. The *bo*'s greater length helped in keeping a swordsman at bay; it could slash like a *naginata* or thrust like a *yari*. He had some close calls early in the match—Musashi's quickness was extraordinary and he would shoot into any opening with the gliding, focused step of a master swordsman—but Katsuyoshi managed, through clever reversals and sweeps, to avoid his opponent's counters.

It was in attempting another maneuver of this sort that he was defeated. As Katsuyoshi thrusted, Musashi slid in along the length of the *bo*. Katsuyoshi began to adjust, preparing for a diagonal strike down across Musashi's shoulder—the cut known as *kesa-giri*. By retracting the *bo* in his movement, he was forced to readjust his grip. Musashi darted a feint to Katsuyoshi's hand. Katsuyoshi jerked his arm out of the way and attempted to regain the momentum of the attack, but the stutter in technique was telling. The strike was not as decisive as it should have been; Musashi caught the shaft in the crossed-sword block known as *juji-dome*, forced the staff down and pivoted around to bring his *bokken* slicing in an arc that stopped just short of his opponent's neck. Katsuyoshi was frantically trying to regain his balance, and even though Musashi had spun into his *shikaku*—the blind spot just outside the range of his peripheral vision—Katsuyoshi's senses were strung to an almost unbearable tension and he could clearly hear the soft moan of Musashi's sword as it cut toward him.

He half expected the explosion of the finishing blow: Musashi had killed men in matches of this type before, even using a *bokken*. But it never came. The bug-eyed swordsman seemed content with his victory as it was.

Katsuyoshi, knelt, breathing heavily, and bowed to Musashi. "*Maitta*." The phrase was so hateful to say—I am beaten—that it had a tight, croaking sound in the stillness of the morning.

Musashi merely nodded, striding over to place his weapons in their bag. He turned as he was adjusting his *daisho* in his sash. It was usual for the victor, in a position of superior status, to bring the meeting to a close. Katsuyoshi sat, his ears burning in shame, at a complete loss. It was well-known that Musashi accepted no disciples. Deep down, Katsuyoshi still believed he could best the bug-eyed swordsman and his pride kept him from begging to become Musashi's disciple. He did not want to learn from this man; he wanted to destroy him.

Musashi's head popped up as these thoughts shot through Katsuyoshi's head. Standing there, looming above him, Musashi looked directly at his opponent with narrowed eyes and said. "No. Do not even think of it. There is no point in another duel. I would kill you then. To have a weapon be inadequate is one thing. When man and weapon are inadequate is quite another."

With these cutting words, he strode off. The witnesses trailed after him, like so many grave ducks. Katsuyoshi rose to his feet, and although he felt the warmth of the sun as it edged over the rim of the hills, his heart was cold within him.

He left that town as quickly as possible, trying not to be conscious of the knowing glances and soft comments made as he hurried down the road. There was nothing left for him here. His *sensei* had set him on a path that now seemed to have no real point to it. He wandered south. Passers-by saw a silent figure, carrying the well-used weapons and predatory look that usually spelled trouble in local *dojo*. But Katsuyoshi never paused in his wanderings. He stared into the distance with the look of a man who was searching for something that, deep down, he felt would never be found. He sat in a boat taking him to Kyushu, a gray man in a gray rain, tossed about by the waves that seemed to him to be much like life itself: shifting, changing shape, incapable of being tamed. On shore, he wandered up into the hills, his staff in hand. It served as a goad to travel; a reminder of his humiliation.

Perhaps in the heights, he thought, he could see clearer. He labored up, only to find the slopes of Homanzan shrouded in fog. The trees, black and silent in the dimness, dripped water onto the ruins of temples. The buildings slouched on slopes, decayed and canted, the victims, not of catastrophe, but of neglect. They were empty mouths gaping into the uncaring night.

Finally, his flight came to an end, not because he had arrived, but because he no longer felt that a destination actually existed. He was empty. Of ambition. Of energy. Alone on the fog-bound hillside, he gazed into the twilight, staring sightlessly at the decayed temple statues known as *jizo*. They stared back.

Eventually, he slept.

Once again, in his dreams, he fought. In a mountain dell, studded with rocks and the dead branches of trees, a young fighter—a boy—attacked. He was silent in assault, smiling faintly, his black eyes glittering with a type of amusement. Again and again, Katsuyoshi attempted to bring his staff to bear, only to have his attacks thwarted.

He burned.

But try as he might, there was no defeating this maddening boy. In the close quarters of the ravine, the staff was too long, his attempts too clumsy. His growing fury choked him until, with a check and a sudden twist of his opponent's hips, Katsuyoshi was thrown down.

The boy pinned one of Katsuyoshi's hands, still gripping the staff, to the ground. The victor stood, gazing down, the point of his sword in the defeated man's face.

"Katsuyoshi." he said, "you must learn to let go."

The sword arced up and then down toward Katsuyoshi's pinned forearm. The blade rang as it sliced through arm and staff.

The sound, still ringing in his head, woke him from his dream.

Letting go. A strange dream. A stranger message. He sat, gazing at his hand, running it over the staff, until the night grew grayer by degrees and morning came.

He was by nature a practical man—a lifetime in the martial arts had shaped him in that regard. But here, on the mountain, where the ghosts of worshipers seemed to slip in and out of the fog-bound ruins of the mountain temples, it was all too easy to believe in a more complicated reality filled with portents in dreams. The very air seemed to lend credence to the tales of the *yamabushi*, the magic monks of the remote hills, renowned masters of the darker aspects of the martial arts. Or of the mythical beings known as *tengu*, who on occasion appeared to supplicants to reveal their combat secrets. In a place where the fog dappled forms and obscured the hard edges of shapes, it seemed to Katsuyoshi that his dream was something more than it appeared.

Letting go. What was the message here? He couldn't completely shake the effects of his training, so he tended to think in largely martial terms. Was he supposed to use only one hand? Would that have saved him from the awful ringing of the *katana* as it sliced through his arm? But the staff was too long to manage that way.

One handed. By letting go, the dream seemed to say, he would avoid defeat and the awful maiming that would ruin him as a warrior. But how could he do so? He relived his duel with Musashi, the way in which the nature of the *bo*—its length usually such an advantage in a duel—had worked against him. Musashi, he now realized, had used his reliance on the staff's length to defeat him. It was in the stuttering moment where he had needed to realign his hold on the shaft that Musashi had driven his attack home.

Length. . . Letting go . . .

Katsuyoshi descended from the hills with a new weapon. A shaft of oak shorter than the *bo*, it retained some of its advantages in reach but, because it stretched only to his shoulders, it was far more manageable. The *jo*, as Katsuyoshi termed it, was quicker to use in reversals, could be deftly shortened and extended. It would be managed with one hand as the fighter adjusted to shifting lines of attack and defense. It permitted him to let go.

He now churned up the turnpikes of central Japan with a new purpose. *Bushi* wise enough to read the balance in his gait and the look in his eye avoided him. What was unusual for Katsuyoshi, however, was that the implicit challenges of less seasoned, more foolish, swordsmen were totally ignored. The man who had in times past sought out all comers as a way of proving himself over and over again seemed, like his weapon, to have been subtly altered.

He and Musashi met after the seasons had wheeled them into the cusp between autumn and the dark grip of winter. The stubble of the field in which they met had been trampled down by the press of weather. Their breath smoked in the cold dawn, the clouds of vapor lit up by the rising sun, emanations of *ki* that billowed out, flashed golden, and were torn apart by the chill wind.

The clash was colder, crisper, harder than their last match. Musashi's force was almost overwhelming, his eyes bugging hungrily as he slashed and whirled at Katsuyoshi. It was, in many ways, more terrifying than the dream that had haunted Katsuyoshi all those months ago.

And yet he was possessed of a type of calm. An observer would almost say he looked remote, except for the fact that the high level of weapons play demanded a vital connection with the here and now. With the *jo* in his hands, Katsuyoshi met Musashi's attacks, gave way and advanced, with a cold focus that made even the Two Sword Man take notice.

This time, it was Musashi who ended up in the dirt. He lay there, breathing heavily and waiting for the final blow from the new weapon that Katsuyoshi wielded so effectively. The cold, brittle earth held him up, as if to offer him to his opponent.

But there was no strike. Katsuyoshi backed away carefully, bowed, and walked quietly away like a man in a dream. He gave Musashi only a fleeting thought—"Now, perhaps, he will know what it is to burn."

Then Katsuyoshi set out for home. He needed to present himself to his *sensei*. To tell them he had learned that, for all those years, when he had grasped his weapons so tightly, so intent on winning, on proving himself, he had in fact been overlooking the most essential lesson: letting go.

There is a significant challenge for human beings in the act of fighting. As biological organisms with the essential purpose of surviving and reproducing, the ability to respond to aggression, or display it ourselves, runs very deep. All living things share this propensity. Yet for people, the whole thing is even more complicated than merely just fighting for survival—killing or being killed. As members of the species *homo sapiens*—"wise" or "knowing" man—we bring a consciousness of the import of our actions to each struggle. In other words, in addition to being involved in a struggle for survival, we have the capacity for knowing what its implications are. And for worrying about it.

Certainly this was one of the things that attracted the feudal *samurai* to the study of Zen Buddhism. Much of Zen seemed to be oriented around combating that sort of reflective consciousness. Through the process of meditation, pupils of Zen learn to let conscious thought "bubble off" and free the individual to experience the here and now with little or no interference from the conscious mind. Certainly one of the things that attracted swordsmen like Yagyu Munenori to Zen was the idea that, by doing away with the sort of worry and thought that defines human beings as sapient, warriors could improve their reflex action and, consequently, their ability to survive.

A real test of an individual's accomplishment in any area is to require him or her to perform in moments of great stress. The notion that you can truly measure someone's character through the way they act in the crucible of extraordinary events is a widely accepted one. It is also one of the reasons why human beings are so interested in stories of heroism—the courage of a soldier on a battlefield, the daring act of rescue, the mother's tenacious defense of her young. For the warriors of Japan, the true test of their progress in Zen was considered to be the way in which they faced the ultimate challenge of life and death embodied in combat.

A great deal has been made of the seemingly suicidal dimension of the warrior's code known as *bushido*. The morbid fascination of Westerners with the act of ritual suicide properly known as *seppuku* (but often coarsely termed *hara kiri*, "belly cutting") or the willingness of Japanese fighters to die for seemingly pointless reasons (fueled by Pacific War veterans' remembrance of the appalling futility of "*banzai* charges") masks the essential reason why Japanese fighters were adamant in their insistence that the warrior must be able to transcend a concern with living in order to reach full fighting potential.

Part of this ideal was, of course, shaped by political reasons. Any army has to indoctrinate its soldiers in an ideology that celebrates the performance of duty under hazardous conditions. It also has to convince the individual fighter that there is something more important than his life—honor, duty, country to cite an American example. And, of course, considerations of these type were part and parcel of the Japanese fighting man's beliefs.

In addition to these more pragmatic considerations, however, the Japanese martial tradition is relatively unique in its incorporation of more philosophically elevated concepts. In this case, Buddhism's conviction that life as we generally perceive it is a type of illusion, and Zen's insistence that the individual could come to enlightenment through the abandonment of a mind-set that made distinctions between the self and other, between subject and object, encouraged Japanese warriors to develop an ideology that encouraged a disregard for death. In this instance, warriors were encouraged not to fear death, not just because it was militarily functional, but because such a mind set, exhibited at critical moments on the battlefield, was dramatic proof the extent to which the individual had internalized the lessons of Zen.

In more civil times, the Japanese acknowledged that the crucible of combat was not a practical way to evaluate enlightenment. Yet, they felt, the combative aspect of the martial arts was so vitally important that it should be preserved in some way. The martial tradition, they felt, was ultimately of value due to its ability to train the human body *and* the spirit. This is, of course, what lies behind the emphasis in the term commonly used for the modern martial arts—*budo* (martial ways).

The masters who adapted martial systems to fit the needs of contemporary trainees were nonetheless aware that they could rob *budo* of some of its intrinsic worth by eliminating the combat experience. If, as Japanese thinkers maintained, *budo* was a type of *seishin tanren* (spiritual forging), then surely a forge with all the heat bled out of it would be of little use to further generations of martial artists.

Traditionally, Japanese martial systems had utilized structured training through a fixed sequence of actions embodied in *kata*. The predictability of *kata* permitted a refinement of technique and created a safety cushion for training with bladed weapons. Yet, during the feudal era, these trainees would also be truly tested outside the precincts of the *dojo* in the lethal environment of the battlefield.

With the pacification of Japan in the seventeenth century, opportunities for true combat testing dwindled. Individual warriors could engage in single duels, as was the case with Katsuyoshi and Musashi, but these activities became increasingly difficult to arrange and were eventually banned by law.

Yet the masters were wary of doing away with all combat. Some martial arts schools, it is true, emphasized training exclusively through forms, but many senior *sensei* decried this as "flowery fighting." If you were teaching someone to fight (even in theory), they maintained, you still needed them to fight.

This led to the institutionalization of various types of free fighting in the modern martial arts forms. Swordsmen had long used wooden training weapons to minimize injuries, and continued to create innovative mock swords that could be used in sparring. The various types of *shinai* used today by *kendoka,* some *aikidoka*, and others, represent good examples of non-lethal weapons that can aid in keeping all the heat (but little of the blood) in contemporary training.

But by eliminating one type of danger, the masters inadvertently introduced another. Non-lethal encounters are, of course, contests. Contests have winners and losers. In the thrill of victory, the rush of pleasure in winning a tournament match, there is a danger of enlarging, not diminishing, the ego. A martial artist infatuated with competition must be on guard not to lose sight of the ultimate purpose of the martial ways.

Katsuyoshi's experience is a case in point. Here is a brilliant martial artist who has mastered the technical aspects of his craft, who has beaten countless opponents, and who has missed the point entirely. For this man, the martial way had ceased to be a path to spiritual development and instead had deteriorated into a means of personal aggrandizement.

So his *sensei* sent him out into the world, hoping that he would suffer defeat and, in the heat of that crucible, have his spirit strengthened.

That process of spiritual forging was an extraordinarily painful process for a proud man like Katsuyoshi. It led him to depression and despair, isolation and doubt. Yet for some reason (perhaps just the habit of training and the need, in all this confusion, to hold onto something familiar), he continued to seek an answer through his training.

An eventually, of course, he found it. We may assume that his teachers saw the potential for enlightenment slumbering deep within him. Yet when it comes, enlightenment arrives in an unexpected way and bearing a confusing message.

For Katsuyoshi's enlightenment comes in a dream. Today, many students of the mind look for insights and messages in dreams that remain hidden from us by the light of day. People of Katsuyoshi's time believed significant dream experiences to have a supernatural origin, and he eventually named his system of fighting with the *jo* Shindo Muso Ryu—the martial tradition of the spirit way dream.

Certainly part of this dream had a technical component that led to the creation of the *jo*. But, we may ask, what else was transmitted? What would have allowed a once-proud warrior, publicly humiliated with his reputation in tatters, to once again confront Musashi with a new, untried system of fighting?

In essence, he had learned to heed the advice of the Spirit Boy in his dream. He had let go. Of pride. Of concern for his reputation. Of the fear of losing. Katsuyoshi had ceased to be haunted by the dream of defeat and became so focused on pursuing total excellence with his new art that he had achieved the state so valued by Zen masters and martial artists alike—*mushin*.

The lesson here for contemporary *budoka*—particularly those active in competitive arts—is to be aware of the spiritual danger inherent in this sort of activity. I am not implying that sparring and various types of matches should be abandoned. I believe that the masters who insisted on their development had some very good reasons for doing so. I am maintaining, however, that, human nature being what it is, there is a real risk that too much of a psychic investment in competition may be ultimately harmful for a sincere pursuit of the martial ways.

The trainee should always be aware that any contest is merely a means to an end. If we vie with one another to test our skills in the heat of a ritual type of combat, it is because we are seeking to test just how well we have internalized the precepts of our arts. We are not (or should not be) there solely for the psychic gratification of winning. In any real sense this would be foolish. No individual wins all the time. We have good days and bad days. Certainly as we age, speed and strength decline. To appreciate sparring only when we win is to effectively rob ourselves of enjoying many of our free fighting experiences.

It is true that the martial artist competing in tournaments will observe many students who have forgotten this lesson. The *kendo* student intent on perfecting technique and pursuing an accurate vision of the art will not always be the most successful of tournament players. She will come across highly competitive *kendoka* who specialize in scoring at all costs, often at the expense of classical technique. Generally speaking, senior *kendo sensei* are quite sensitive to matters of tradition and technique, but in the speed and heat of contests, the sound of an accurate hit alone (since the *shinai* often moves too quickly for the eye to follow) can result in a point. Tournament players know this, and so work to truncate their techniques for maximum speed and tournament effectiveness. In doing so, of course, they move their *kendo* further and further away from its martial roots, and, should they persevere in their studies, lay the groundwork for a spiritual crisis in later years.

The ethical lesson in Katsuyoshi's tale, then, and in the quality of *mushin*, is to exert care lest our pursuit of the martial arts becomes just another way of feeding the ego instead of a way of conquering it. To follow the martial path correctly (that is, ethically) we need to constantly keep in mind the real purpose of training.

I am reminded of a group of *kendo* trainees I was with who were discussing their recent meeting with a Japanese national champion. They were all active competitors who were mesmerized by the speed and skill of the champion. What, they asked, was the secret of his training?

There is no secret, he told them. You just need to remember to strive always to make your *kendo* beautiful. Not fast. Not flashy. Only beauty matters. Everything else will follow.

That man was a champion, not because he grasped his *shinai* tightly, but because he was so focused on the perfection of the art that he had learned to let go.

ZANSHIN

Sound. Stillness. Each with a message.

In the hush of the garden, the remote hum of the city was kept at bay. The dry rasp of calloused feet on the wood floor, the faint rustle of the *hakama* were magnified. The bamboo shafts rattled briefly as Shiro set himself in the ritual that was *kyudo*. The tidal wash of breathing began as he settled into the focus of his art. The bow, arching above his head, and the target became linked.

Thrummm. The arrow sped on its way.

The pattern begins again. *Thrummm.*

Again. *Thrummm.*

Thrummm.

Thud! The rhythm of the sound pulls him back ten years. The sounds are harsher, but as regular. *Thud!* The hiss of breath, the moment where time seems to stop as the interplay of speed and technique and balance are measured in the blink of an eye. Then the sound—*thud!*—As bone and muscle crash into the mat.He is back in the Kodokan.

No solitary ritual there, no measured ceremony of placement. An elegance, yes, but an elegance of a different order. The nervous shuffle and sweep of feet as fighters waited for a chance on the mat. The tight, coiling moves as players rehearsed technique. The bright eyes watching, measuring, probing for weaknesses. The sweat. The bone-crushing slam to the mat. The lethal darting for the choke hold.

The joy of the champion.

Shida Shiro, it was said, was born to study *jujutsu*. In late nineteenth century Japan, hundreds of schools of unarmed combat flourished as the nation entered the modern era, determined to both preserve its past and enter its rightful place in the world as a progressive leader. *Jujutsu dojo* were flooded with trainees and, in the heat of competition between students and between schools, a vicious type of selection went on where only the quickest and hardiest could endure.

Shiro was naturally quick. He had an almost reflexive ability to respond to his opponent's moves. Although never huge, he thickened over the course of the years, seeming to grow a protective layer of muscle to cushion the falls, fight off the twisting of his joints, and give him that extra edge that spelled the difference between defeat and victory.

As a youth, he had his share of humiliations. His step-father, Saigo Tanomo, was not a gentle man. He had a ruthless drive within him to elevate his *jujutsu* to the pinnacle of the martial arts world. He saw within Shiro the raw material to effect this, and he pushed the boy mercilessly

And so Shiro grew, almost unthinking, into a champion. He was pushed along by the drive of his elder's ambition, helpless in the pull of his duty as a son. Nor was the relationship entirely one-sided. His step-father, custodian of the secret technique of *oshiki-uchi*, had armed Shiro with a combination of finesse and fury, making him the jewel of the *dojo*.

In his skill and youth, Shiro tended to disregard his opponents. He took them seriously, of course—in his father's *dojo* every bout was to be treated as if it were *shinken shobu*, a match with real swords, a fight to the death—but gave little thought to the bodies he left groaning on the mat. Shiro trained himself into a type of weapon and, like a weapon, he was capable of no real thought about his targets.

Yet deep within Shiro there was something that yearned for more than the single-minded pursuit of his father's *jujutsu*. He would have been hard pressed to give name to it and, indeed, was only fleetingly aware of it on any conscious level. Sometimes in the quiet night after the flush of victory had faded, while his step-father slept, Shiro wondered . . .

Then, he met Professor Kano. Kano Jigoro Sensei was gaining a name for himself as both an educator in the new style as well as someone deeply concerned with preserving what was worthy in Japan's old culture. Kano the educator and Kano the custodian of culture met in his work with *jujutsu*. The Professor had studied a number of different *ryu*. He was not a brilliant competitor like Shiro, but he was persistent, methodical. He trained intensely. It was said you could tell when Kano was coming before you laid eyes on him because of the smell of the liniment he freely spread all over his bruised body.

But in that compact, battered form, there lived a mind of deep complexity and razor sharpness. Kano studied *jujutsu* in a way never done before. He learned the techniques. He analyzed them. He attempted to distill the essence of any movement, to purify it, and make it plain.

Not for the Professor was the mystery of traditional *jujutsu*. As a cultural treasure, he believed the art should be celebrated and explained, not hoarded away and revealed only to an elite few. Above all, Kano was deeply concerned that the practice of martial arts should have an ethical purpose. *Jujutsu*, he felt, should be practiced as *judo*, a "way" that lent depth and meaning to each trainee's life in and out of the *dojo*.

When Professor Kano was received at Shiro's *dojo* with barely concealed hostility, the young man watched his reactions carefully. If Kano noticed the subtle insults directed his way, he gave no indication. He quietly and respectfully told Shiro's father that he had been told of the excellence of the *jujutsu* practiced here and of the remarkable ability of Shiro. He asked only the opportunity to watch the training and to discuss the techniques.

Saigo was not immune to flattery, and Kano was invited to stay. He watched intently, sitting motionless off the mat. Shiro felt the power of Kano's gaze, the sword-like sharpness of his scrutiny.

After training, Kano and Saigo had a brief discussion of some technical points that the Professor raised. Saigo rarely discussed anything about his art, preferring students to learn through hard knocks, but Kano managed to drag the old man into a brief conversation.

"Saigo Sensei," the Professor concluded, "I am inviting the most skilled students of *jujutsu* to my school to help preserve this art for future generations. Would you permit Shiro to come and demonstrate his remarkable technique?" Only the best fighters in Tokyo would be invited, he continued, and it would be an honor if he could include Saigo's star pupil.

Shiro held his breath. Eventually, the persuasive Professor won out over the gruff Saigo.

And so, Shiro entered the Kodokan.

Here the vague unease Shiro felt in the quiet of night was put to rest. Under Kano's tutelage, the new *judoka* were encouraged to think about their art. How is this throw done differently by the different *ryu*? When you stripped away its variations, what was the essence of the technique? What principles does it reveal about movement, human action, purpose?

Kano pinned his students to the mat in more ways than one. His focus was never on winning a match, but on uncovering fundamental principles through action. It was perplexing to Shiro and his fellow students how such a bookish fellow could be fixated so much on principles and yet so skilled on the mat at the same time. It was not unusual for Kano to break off in the middle of a contest and deliver a long, complex, but perfectly lucid discussion of how the contestants had illustrated some interesting points, and how these points could be understood through assiduous training in the following techniques. . .Then Kano would resume his actions. In later years, senior *judoka* would assert that Kano, for all his erudition, was almost impossible to throw down. It was, one pupil asserted, like fighting with an empty jacket—when you tried to execute a technique, there was nothing there.

Principles were in the air of the Kodokan. Kano insisted that it was not enough to be a skilled fighter. To fully practice *budo*, one needed to devote oneself to overarching principles that were equally applicable in the *dojo* and the world outside. He insisted that his students be gentlemen. They were, to be sure, hard fighting and overly athletic gentlemen, but they were gentlemen nonetheless.

For Shiro, this was a new way of looking at things. He embraced Kano's concept of *judo* wholeheartedly and found the ethical and philosophical aspects of the Kodokan as valuable as the tremendously punishing training that was its counterpart. In elevating the art from a type of *jutsu* to a *do*, Shiro had found an answer to many of his nameless problems.

But like many types of enlightenment, this one was not without its painful side. For, in embracing Kano, Shiro had effectively rejected his step-father. At first, he had dutifully attempted to divide his time equally between Saigo's and Kano's training halls. He hoped in this way to hide his growing attachment to his new teacher. What was harder to obscure was the development of his technique. Under Kano's tutelage Shiro seemed to blossom, developing a poise and skill that was only matched by a growing sense of humanity. In Saigo's rough and tumble *dojo*, the technique was welcome. The humanity, however, was decidedly out of place.

Eventually, Shiro came to spend more and more time under the watchful eye of Professor Kano. A sense of duty prevented him from totally abandoning his step-father, but it was clear to all observers where Shiro's real heart rested.

Deep in his heart, Shiro knew he would have to decide. On the increasingly rare occasions when he trained at his step-father's school, he felt the smoldering gaze of Saigo burning just out of sight. Even at the Kodokan, where Shiro came to play an increasingly prominent role as an instructor, he was not immune from a similar scrutiny. Kano would watch from the side of the *tatami*, his eyes keen in an otherwise placid face. Both *sensei* watched their pupil to see which way he would follow.

It came to a head on a steamy summer day in an exhibition hall where the air was as thick and humid as the Tokyo afternoon. Months before, many of the old *jujutsu* masters had grown alarmed at the growing prestige of the Kodokan. The upstart Kano had shrewdly attracted not only extremely able pupils like Shiro, but a number of influential patrons who were advocating that Kano's new system of *judo* become part of the training regimen of the Metropolitan Police. At this, the *jujutsu sensei* exploded in indignation. Finally, it was agreed upon by all concerned that, in the interest of patriotism, a contest should be held. Not to decide whether a form of unarmed combat should be taught, but, rather, which form should be used.

The *jujutsu sensei* sat around tables, sipping *sake*, blunt men who had faced each other in contests over the years. United in their enmity, they grouped together and plotted their strategy. Ultimately, the question was asked.

"Saigo, will Shiro fight for you or the bookworm?"

It was a dangerous question to ask of a man never known for his patience and now not in the best of moods. His reply was remarkably tame: "The excellence of my *dojo* does not hinge on any one man. Shiro will do what he will. My students will beat Kano."

The tournament, when it came, was an exposition of some of the best practitioners of unarmed grappling Japan had ever seen. They lined up to salute the referees at the beginning of the meet, their uniforms as varied as the styles they represented; gray and striped *hakama*, *keikogi* of every conceivable style and color. And, conspicuous in their simplicity, Kano's students bowed to the judges in the white *gi* and black belts he had awarded them. Shiro stood with them.

The hall was a cavernous affair, and the spectators were buzzing with anticipation. Once the tournament began, however, the hall grew silent. The only sounds were from the fighters on the mats: the shuffle of feet, the rasping of breath, the slam of bodies falling, the croak of submission, and the calls of the judges.

As the day wore on, the tension mounted. Clearly, Kano's students were not invincible, but they more than held their own against the challenges Japan's *jujutsu sensei* could throw at them. And it was clear that Shiro was among the best contestants there. Experts watched with narrowed eyes as he moved through match after match, eliminating the weaker contestants. They nodded in silent satisfaction at his skill.

And at the end, it came down to a contest between Shiro and a cropped headed bull of a man, a student of Saigo's, renowned for not only emerging victorious in a string of contests, but for maiming his opponents in the process. The hall had dimmed as the summer sky darkened with the promise of rain. Thunder rumbled ominously in the distance. Lightening flickered on the two fighter's faces as they jerked into the ritual bow before the match began.

The struggle was so rapid, so fluid, that only the most advanced practitioners among the spectators could really follow every nuance. The men feinted, adjusted, jockeyed for dominance in a superheated dance that few in the audience had ever seen before.

Saigo, on the sidelines, grunted and hissed with every move, following the fortunes of his new protégé and his stepson with furious attention. Kano sat, impassive, only his eyes alive to the drama unfolding before him.

Shiro stumbled under a furious attack. A collective gasp rose up as the crowd anticipated a finishing throw. But with the cat-like agility he was known for, Shiro escaped. His opponent, unbalanced by his anticipation of a winning move, backed off for a split second to adjust for a new line of attack. In that split second, Shiro flashed onto the offensive. Using *oshiki-uchi*, he slammed his opponent into the mat and choked him into submission. The hall exploded. Kano stood and across the room his eyes locked onto those of Saigo. The bigger man glanced at Shiro, standing with head bowed, panting, almost disconnected from the tumult around him. An impartial observer would almost say he looked appalled at what he had done. Finally, Saigo turned, stiffly bowed to Kano, and left the hall.

After the closing ceremony, the Kodokan members circled Kano in a jubilant ring. Only Shiro seemed less than elated.

Kano looked him in the eye. Their relationship had become so close that no question needed to be asked. "Sensei," he stammered, "it was *his* technique I used. His."

"Shiro," Kano murmured, "the point is not where we get our gifts, it is what we do with them."

Outside, the rain fell in torrents.

After that day, Shiro could never approach the Kodokan without the feeling that, in using the technique he had mastered in his stepfather's *dojo* to win the day for Kano, he had betrayed both men. He had rejected Saigo's *ryu* for the allure of the Professor's martial way, yet had used Saigo's special technique. He had embraced Kano's system, feeling it superior in every way, yet had, seemingly, abandoned its precepts in the heat of the tournament.

Gripped by a sense of guilt and powerless to break its hold through rationalization, Shiro merely went through the motions of training in *judo*. Finally, unable to bear the conflict within him, and unwilling to give Kano anything but his best, Shiro went to the Professor and announced his intentions to quit *judo* for good.

Kano silently motioned for the young man to sit beside him and spoke carefully and slowly. "Shiro, you are an honorable man. I could argue that you, in fact, acted in the best interest of the martial arts by using all your skills—*all of them*—in the service of a greater good. Because I truly believe that *judo* is a superior way of studying the martial arts of our nation. Your victory will permit us to bring many benefits to the people of this country through training in our art."

Shiro started to speak, but Kano held up his hand. "It is a measure of your goodness that you feel the conflicts you feel. I hope you can find a way to live with yourself. If, however, the burden becomes too great, remember that there are many *do*, many ways to follow in this world.

"I once told you that we are all given gifts, but the most important thing is how we use those gifts. I will now tell you that there are many virtuous ways to use our talents. In some ways it grieves me to say it, but *judo* is not the only way for you. Choose the path you will." Sighing, Kano got up and walked toward the door. "The students need me now."

He paused briefly and, looking for a last time at his pupil, Kano said, "Remember, you will always be my student as long as you follow the way, no matter what form it takes."

Saigo Shiro left Tokyo, unable to reconcile the pull of his two fathers. He moved to Nagasaki, eventually becoming a journalist. As if the memories of *judo* were too painful, Shiro abandoned the art and instead immersed himself in the solitary art of archery. Stripped of the distraction of competition and opponent, Shiro seemed to find solace in *kyujutsu*.

But on some quiet days the rhythm of the bow and the thudding impact of the shaft pulled him back. Almost unbidden, he relived his choices. He reviewed his life's trajectory with all the intensity once displayed on the *judo* mat and with all the cold dispassion of a master archer watching the arrow's flight. On warm quiet evenings, the measured punctuation of *kyujutsu*'s ritual swept him into painful reverie, until he was no longer sure whether what he heard was the thud of the arrow, the sound from that fateful contest reverberating over the years, or merely the beating of his own heart.

Like *judo*, life is a game of balance, of awareness, and of sensitivity to others. In this art, like many others, the concept of *zanshin* is stressed. Literally "remaining mind," this term is often translated as "awareness." But it is awareness of a particular type. It involves the ability to be focused on a technique but not to lose sight of the greater picture. In *judo*, you can demonstrate *zanshin* by maintaining your composure even as you fall, controlling that fall through the art of *ukemi*, and remaining alive to the possibility of countering your opponent's move. In *kendo*, trainees are encouraged to display *zanshin* of a slightly different type by maintaining perfect posture and follow through after a technique and remaining aware of the movements of opponents.

In both cases, trainees are encouraged not to lose themselves in the moment. Focus on actions, yes. Commit fully, of course. Yet, at the same time, the *sensei* seem to be calling for a heightened awareness of a greater sphere of interaction: the relation of the technique and the moment to the wider context of the contest. When we extend the notion of *zanshin* out beyond the confines of the *dojo*, we are warning against all types of self-absorption and advocating an awareness of and sensitivity to the larger context in which we all live our lives.

Shiro's tale is one that shows a master competitor and a martial artist coming alive to the full potentiality of the way. At the same time, he is an individual enmeshed, as are we all, in a complex series of relationships, loyalties and conflicts. For our purposes, the interesting thing about this story is not the recounting of his prowess, but rather the examination of how an extremely well-developed type of *zanshin* led him to a particular series of actions.

The struggle Shiro experienced may seem somewhat minimal to us today. The Japanese, however, have an extreme sensibility to the nuances of human relations, especially those between superiors and subordinates. The concepts of *on*, the deep obligation that a child owes to his or her parents, and of *giri*, the sense of duty that such obligation entails, are extremely powerful. They are rendered even more compelling by the realization that, in real terms, children can never fully repay their parents, and that the process of growing up inevitably makes demands on an individual that can cause conflict with the notion of *giri*.

Such is the case with Shiro. A gifted youth with tremendous potential, he is trained by his step-father in the art of *jujutsu*. Saigo's rationale for doing so may be debated. It could have been for adult self-gratification through the triumphs of a child (familiar to anyone who has come into contact with a particular type of Little League parent) or a genuine attempt to give Shiro something of lasting value, however gruff the giver's demeanor. But this question is insoluble and beside the point. The fact of the matter is that Saigo's training created a tremendous obligation on Shiro's part to honor his mentor.

When Kano enters the scene, the stage is set for an intense type of conflict. Kano Jigoro was erudite, cosmopolitan, highly intelligent—a gentleman in the truest sense. He brought an added dimension to his study of the grappling arts: the conviction that they were structured by an underlying logic, and that the exploration of that elegant logic could be used as a way for cultivating the human spirit. The young athlete Shiro responded to this vision, to Kano's revelation of new and undreamed of horizons. For a time Shiro may have deluded himself into thinking he was only polishing technique by studying with another style of fighting (not an uncommon practice), but ultimately, the vision Kano had for his Kodokan completely seduced the young trainee. And this vision continues to do the same thing for countless trainees today.

But for Shiro, this new and heartfelt allegiance to *judo* created a terrible dilemma. It was made all the more difficult by the very public struggle between the Kodokan and other *jujutsu* schools for preeminence. The moral courage Shiro must have possessed to stand that day in the simple white *gi* of the *judoka*, signaling to all his complete break with his step-father, was enormous. He had, in fact, reached that inevitable day when a grown child chooses his own course of action, often hurting a parent in the process.

But for Shiro the intolerable thing was not his mere choosing of Kano over Saigo; it was in the double offense he had committed in using his step-father's own technique against him. For Shiro, it must have seemed hypocritical. Here he was, making a public display of fidelity to Kano and indicating that he thought the Professor's system was superior, and yet using the techniques of another style—his step-father's—to prove this dominance.

You could rationalize the action away, of course. The heat of the contest. A sudden reflexive action, not a conscious thought. Kano's system really a synthesis of many styles, no real betrayal in using this technique. Kano probably attempted something of that type as is indicated in the story. But for Shiro, this seemed an almost overwhelming violation of the respect he owed his step-father.

And, as always with the Japanese, the question was how to make amends for this violation.

We know Shiro's solution. In many ways, abandoning *judo* would not take back the hurt of his actions. It would, however, ensure that nothing of that type could ever happen again. And, as far as we know, Shiro never went back to a *judo dojo* again.

Imagine the sacrifice that must have entailed. Many of us training in the martial arts have developed a real attachment to them. There is something about them—the physical activity, the mental challenge, the spiritual gratification, the shared purpose—we crave. To give them up would be almost unthinkable; a painful process at best.

How much more wrenching must Shiro's decision have been? He was not just an enthusiastic trainee. He was one of the greatest grapplers in Japan. Ahead of him stretched a bright future. As Kano's premier student and chief instructor, Shiro's fame and fortune would grow with that of the Kodokan. A man blessed in being able to follow his avocation and to gain security and respect through his performance, he threw it all away.

But, as another thinker once asked, what does it avail someone to gain a fortune and lose the soul? For Shiro, the only honorable choice was to forsake the art he loved, to sacrifice an aspect of his personal happiness for something even more important. Obligation and duty sound like such harsh things, but the very strength of the words underscores their importance.

For, whether we like it or not (and Shiro's story indicates that there may well be times when we do not) we are bound in a whole host of ties and relations to other human beings. Our actions impact not only on ourselves, but on a wide network of people. And because this is the case, we need to scrutinize the tenor of our actions, to impose the harsh, critical gaze of the *sensei* on what we do, in the *dojo* and out. And when we find that what we do, however convenient or pleasurable, does not quite measure up to the highest standards, we have on obligation to change our behavior, no matter how distasteful that may be.

Shiro's story, in many ways, is a case study of heroism. Not because he achieved greatness in *judo*, but because, having reached that pinnacle, he was willing to abandon it in pursuit of a higher standard of behavior.

Zanshin.

5. Meditation and Action

Which brings us to the end of our discussion and to a final nagging question. Granted that the purpose of the martial arts is to make us better, more moral, people. But how to define what these morals are? What do we mean by better?

It is one of the more frustrating elements of Zen that the masters are relatively cryptic on this point. Modern martial artists tend to be somewhat evasive as well. And their reticence is understandable: in pluralistic societies, it is possible for different martial artists to have very different notions about right and wrong, about faith, and belief, and human purpose. Yet I believe that the serious pursuit of these arts enmeshes the trainee in a significant human conversation, one that stretches over centuries and across continents, and one that is concerned precisely with issues of ultimate human purpose.

Indeed, much of this book is an exploration of this theme and what it implies. Which means that, if the implication is accepted, we need to begin to demarcate at least the broad boundaries of right behavior that we can all agree on.

It is a truism that the martial arts emphasize both meditation and action. Yet, despite the fact that this is a type of platitude, it doesn't hurt to point this out: these two things are highly useful endeavors. Perhaps, by using a different emphasis, by pursuing the two types of action in slightly different ways, we may be able to begin the process of teasing out what I mean when I write about the moral dimension of the martial arts.

On one level, meditation can be the means through which we quiet our minds and strive for the characteristic of no-mind that the Zen masters valued so highly. It also has the connotation, however, of reflection or serious thought. And the less obvious interpretation is the one I would like to explore. Reflection and serious thought may be the first steps toward a moral dimension to the martial arts.

The kind of activity I have in mind is very often a difficult one. Thought—serious thought—is, I am afraid to say, an activity increasingly rare in contemporary society. You have only to look at the nature of what passes for political debate today, the abysmal academic performance of many of our young people, rampant consumerism, and the series of social ills that seem to beset us on every hand, to get the sense that intense reflection is not a regular part of many people's lives. And despite a certain smugness on our part, martial artists (products of that culture) are no better. For, in the final analysis, we have to admit that many martial artists, despite giving lip service to the *do* aspect of their practice, tend to be more interested in the physical exercises of the their disciplines rather than the spiritual ones.

Part of this may have to do with the fact that this kind of inner exploration is also often immensely painful. Martial arts training is, in many ways, a microcosmic version of the reflection all human beings need in their lives. Pause and think about this. Training involves things like subordination to a system, the ability to defer immediate gratification, the willingness to endure things like discomfort, pain, the possibility of looking foolish in front of your peers, and the humiliation of defeat. Its saving grace is that all these things are accepted in the name of a greater good.

Self-reflection is like that. It requires us to think with a great deal of focus and clarity on the how's and why's of our lives. What am I doing? Why? What is the ultimate point? And, most importantly, it requires us to ask the very painful question about whether our life has some transcendent purpose. And by transcendent, I mean one that is oriented not merely around self-gratification, but that has some larger purpose in view.

These are difficult questions to ask. Which is why many spiritual traditions insist on the importance of a teacher, a mentor, a confessor, a guide. Or a *sensei*. One of the lessons the Oxherding Pictures transmits to us is that human beings, while driven to ask themselves the important questions, are also capable of almost infinite self-delusion and evasion. Like all biological organisms, we tend to shy away from pain and seek out pleasure. The wise will maintain that, despite the pain involved, such an inner search leads to much more profound rewards than immediate gratification. The wise (who are not so called without justification) are also well aware, however, that imposing the type of self-discipline necessary to walk such a spiritual path is often beyond the ability of most people, especially when they are in the early stages of their search.

So the teacher's job is to keep the seeker on the right path. The teacher guides and encourages. In martial arts terms, by virtue of his or her example, the *sensei* shows us that, despite the seemingly impossible demands a martial art places on us, despite the feeling that we will never be able to master its techniques, such achievement *is* possible.

Of course, the good teacher is as much a goad as an example. As a result, good teachers are hated as much as they are loved. For a large part of the teacher's obligation is not just concerned with praising us when we do well. Good teachers also ask the hard questions of us. Hold forth almost impossible standards of excellence. And hold us to them. They teach us, in short, how to herd the ox. They demand from us the type of single heartedness we know as *isshin*.

Now, what action is required of us as we pursue this path of self-reflection? In the martial arts, the obvious answer is training. We must put into movement the lessons we have internalized. Yet there is another, more important, dimension to this call to action.

We are, once again, at something of a dilemma here due to the heterogeneous backgrounds of martial artists all over the world. A call to action beyond the exercise of mere technique in the *dojo* is problematic. Yet, if my contention regarding a higher purpose to training is right, certainly we must be able to establish some commonality of purpose in our studies.

First, let us dispense with the ridiculous notion that we seek mastery only because of the fighting skills it imparts. I will grant you that there are people who train in martial arts disciplines only for this reason, but they are not on the road to mastery. Somehow, they got sidetracked to a worship of aggression and dominance. They have been deluded into thinking that the victory they may experience in the ring is something more than a game, an abstraction. It may be impressive, but it is impressive in only one small facet of human potentiality. If it is not somehow translated into something more expansive, it is not so much glorious as it is pathetic. Even the Romans, who seemed to possess greatness and venality in almost equal proportions, assigned a slave to accompany their heroes in victory parades. And that slaves job was to whisper into the victor's ear that all glory is fleeting. Any time we get too carried away with our skills, we need to listen for that whisper.

So. What is the point? And, more importantly, what is the point that we can agree on together? A fairly erudite thinker once stated that, although human cultures are wondrously diverse, all peoples seemed to value two things: work and love. Perhaps we can start there.

Why is work so important to people? Notice that what is valued is not just "activity" or even "creativity," but work. Work involves activity and often creativity, it is true. But it is also activity and creativity that is somehow linked to others, to a wider social grouping. We work to produce things or services that somehow link us to other people. And to engage in this activity, we are required to cooperate, to impose a type of discipline on ourselves. Even people who enjoy their jobs are not always happy about working. And, certainly, vast numbers of people maintain that they do not enjoy their jobs at all. Yet researchers often reveal the fact that many people find their jobs deeply rewarding, not necessarily just because they produce the wherewithal needed to survive, but because they connect people to other people, they contribute toward our sense of identity and self worth, and they give us an enhanced purpose in life.

The microcosm of the *dojo* does the same thing. It enmeshes us in a social universe that can generate a sense of community and common purpose. It demands that we place ourselves under discipline and (certainly in more traditional arts and training halls) demands a real subordination of our individualism in the name of something greater.

The challenge in making martial training a martial art is to take these insights and transfer them to the other dimensions of our own lives. Are we aloof? Smug? Superior in the self-complacency of our training? It is a very real danger that we may tend to invest more energy into our martial arts training than in the totality of our lives, and we need to remain aware of this.

I'll use myself as an example. I have a fairly responsible job at a small college. It demands a great deal of my energy and, sometimes, inordinate amounts of my time. At the same time, I train in the martial arts. I am also a husband and the father of two children. When the stress of the job increases, I am often irritable, and distant and withdrawn at home. It often seems as if I expend most of my energy on things other than home life. Yet I usually manage to dredge up enough energy to go the *dojo*. Once, after a successful promotion *shiai* in *kendo*, I was all pumped up and animated. My wife cut me sort with one curt sentence: "Great. Just one more thing to feed your head."

There are many different types of *sensei*.

What my wife was trying to tell me was not just that she was exasperated that I was so grumpy and listless about things at home and full of disgusting energy when it came to *kendo*, but that I had somehow gotten off track. By thinking too much of myself and not of others, I had displayed an appalling lack of *mushin*. For no-mind refers not only to the action state we seek in sparring; it more importantly hints at the need to let go of an all-consuming concern with the self and focus on something greater. We should train for life, not live so that we can train. If we are not equally involved and committed to our lives in the wider social nexus, we have failed in our search for a way.

So, the lesson the martial arts seems to be sending us is that we should strive for connections beyond ourselves, to become enmeshed in relations with others. I will leave it up to the reader to best decide where that relationship can be formed. I can suggest the family, the community, the school, a political party, a place of worship, and leave it up to individual choice and circumstance. I will maintain, however, that the community of the *dojo* is not sufficient.

The second thing that all people seem to value is love. I am not naive enough to believe that all societies everywhere have the same notions regarding the many different types of love. Romantic love, in particular, is a somewhat problematic concept in many cultures all over the world. But all peoples everywhere honor some type of emotional connection between people (the bond between mothers and children is a widespread example).

Widely construed, the quality of *zanshin* seems to hint at the need for connection. In strictly technical terms, it indicates that the martial artist needs to be connected to his or her surroundings, the environment of the encounter, which includes people, as well as physical and psychic conditions. It also stresses the need not to lose that sense of awareness, even in the most intense and focused moments when we execute technique.

The masters seem to be suggesting that martial arts training is a way to help us cope with the world, and that it would be highly ironic if, through our training, we somehow got so engrossed in the minutia of our coping mechanism that we lost sight of its ultimate purpose.

The ultimate purpose must, in some way, be about the maintenance and fostering of ties between human beings. I have always thought it interesting that the ideograph for *jin* (benevolence or mercy) is created by using the radical for person and the symbol for two, stressing the fact that this highly important Confucian virtue is about the proper relationship between people.

I would maintain that the martial arts, by attempting to give us some control over our bodies and minds, by equipping us to deal with stresses of a variety of types, is a mechanism to foster *jin*. The art of *aikido*, for instance, emphasizes the fact that, through training, the individual can learn to redirect an attacker's energy and, by eliminating the threat of harm, permit the defender to deal with his attacker in a truly humane way. Put less technically, mastery and control foster self-confidence and poise. Such individuals have a greater likelihood of responding appropriately to crises, threats, and the continuing series of unexpected trials that make up a human life.

Our training, by freeing us from fears and anxiety, also equips us for the challenge of human interaction. Training does this by establishing a paradigm to guide us in our lives. The *dojo* teaches us to respect and value the experiences of others, to engage in constant self-reflection and improvement, and to strive for lofty goals. At the same time, the *dojo* presents us with a concrete structure to pursue these activities. Above all, it teaches us that some of the most rewarding things are also some of the most difficult things to master. And that they are also the most worthwhile.

If we can bring this conviction and this paradigm into the broader arena of our social lives, we will have made significant strides toward transforming our arts into ways.

Above all, we need to keep the martial arts in perspective. They are (or can be) *ways* to something, not the thing itself. They are, in short, a category of tool. As such, they can be utilized for good purposes or bad. It is my conviction that the dynamics involved in learning a martial art are ones that are extremely effective and exert an emotive pull on people because, in many ways, they mimic the process of spiritual discovery that each human being yearns for in the deepest recesses of the heart. But this doesn't mean that practicing an art alone is a good and sufficient response to this yearning.

As the Oxherding Pictures indicate, the type of activity involved in training is designed to bring us somewhere, to achieve a transformation and provide us with a revelation. Once we arrive at that event, however, we have really only begun our journey. It is then up to each of us to choose how we will use our experience to meet the challenge of being fully human.

Which means, of course, that I am following the lead of countless teachers in the Zen and martial traditions by presenting the reader, not with a prescription for behavior, but for some broad suggestions that each person needs to explore for his or her self:

Endeavor.

Ask the tough questions and don't shy away when you get some tough answers.

Seek perfection.

Remember to embrace your discipline tightly, but other people tighter still.

Train well.

Text References

· Chan Wing-tsit

1963. *The Platform Scripture*. Jamaica: St. John's University Press

Donohue, John J.

1994. *Warrior Dreams: The Martial Arts and the American Imagination*. Westport: Bergin and Garvey.

1993. "Social Organization and Martial Systems: A Cross-Cultural Typology." *Journal of Asian Martial Arts*, Vol. 2, no. 1:40-51.

1991. *The Forge of the Sapirit: Structure, Motion and Meaning in the Japanese Martial Tradition*. New York: Garland Publishing.

1990. "Training Halls of the Japanese Martial Tradition: A Symbolic Analysis of *Budo Dojo* in New York." *Anthropos* Vol. 85:55-63.

1988. "Sword Magic: Belief, Form, and Function in the J Japanese Martial Tradition." *Human Affairs* Vol. 14:9-35.

Draeger, Donn.
1974. *Modern Bujutsu and Budo*. New York: John Weatherhill.

Harris, Victor
1974. *A Book of Five Rings: Miyamoto Musashi* Woodstock: The Overlook Press.

Legget, Trevor
1978. *Zen and the Ways*. London: Routledge and Kegan Paul

Nicol, C. W.
1975. *Moving Zen: Karate as a Way to Gentleness* New York: Quill

Sato Hiroaki (trans.)
1986. *The Sword and the Mind* Woodstock: The Overlook Press.

Stevens, John
1984. *Sword of No Sword: Life of the Master Warrior Tesshu*. Boston: Shambhala Press.

Suzuki, D.T.
1959. *Zen and Japanese Culture*. Princeton: Princeton University Press.

Wilson, William Scott (trans.)
1979. *Hagakure: The Book of the Samurai* Tokyo: Kodansha International, Ltd.

Glossary

aikido - "way of harmony," a modern *budo* form which emphasizes spiritual mastery for the development of technical proficiency in its throws, locks, and immobilizations

aikidoka - one who practices *aikido*

aiki-jutsu - the combat-oriented precursor of *aikido*

bakufu - tent government, term used to describe a military dictatorship

batsugun - judo competitor who has scored twenty or more victories in contests

bo - six foot wooden staff used as a weapon in *karate* and other martial arts

bogu - *kendo* armor

bokken - also rendered *bokuto*, a wooden training sword

budo - martial ways

budoka - martial arts practitioner

bujutsu - martial techniques

bushi - warrior

bushido - warriors code, the philosophy surrounding the practice of the martial arts

daimyo - great names, the lords of feudal Japan

dan - category used to describe the rank of advanced practitioners in many martial arts forms

do - way or path

do - chest protector used in *kendo*

dojo - training hall

dojo kun - *dojo* precepts, often recited at the close of practice sessions

gi - training uniform consisting of jacket and trousers

hakama - pleated, divided skirt worn in some Japanese martial arts forms

hanshi - master

hara - lower abdomen, the center of the body where *ki* is focused

haragei - form of intuition

iaido - modern martial art which teaches the use of the Japanese sword through a series of solo exercises

iemoto - voluntary corporate group based upon Japanese kinship model

isshin - "one-mind," singleheartedness

jin - benevolence

jiu-jutsu - also *ju-jutsu*, "techniques of gentleness" the combat-oriented predecessor of judo

jiyu-renshu - free fighting in kendo

jo - a hardwood short staff approximately fifty inches long

judo - gentle way, a modern martial arts form based on empty-hand techniques which emphasize throwing, wrestling, and a variety of other techniques

judogi - *judo* practice uniform

judoka - one who practices *judo*

jujutsu - techniques of gentility

jutsu - system of techniques

kama - a sickle used in weapons training

kami - a term used to identify the gods of the Shinto pantheon, its literal meaning is "superior"

kamiza - deity seat, the shrine of the *dojo*

kan - hall, a name used to identify a martial arts school

karate - empty-hand fighting system which utilizes strikes, kicks, and blocks with the hands, feet, and other parts of the body; further classified as *karate-do* (the way of karate) which has pronounced philosophical overtones and *karate-jutsu* (*karate* techniques), which is more combat-oriented

kata - stylized sequence of techniques used in martial arts training

katana - Japanese long sword

katsujinken - the sword that gives life, part of a motto of Yagyu swordsmen

keiko - practice

keikogi - another term for practice uniform

ken zen ichi mi - the goals of the sword and that of zen are the same, a kendo training motto
kendo - "way of the sword," a modern Japanese martial art based on sword techniques of feudal Japan
kendoka - one who practices *kendo*
kenjutsu - sword techniques, Japanese fencing
kenshi - swordsman
ki - universal energy
kiai - shout used in training to express and help foster the unity of mind, body, and ki
kime - focus
kirakaeshi - repetition of kendo strokes
koan - seemingly insoluble riddles used in Zen to propel a student into enlightenment
kobudo - literally "old martial ways," it is often used to refer to weapons training in karate
kote - protective mitts which form part of *kendo* armor
kumite - sparring
kung fu - popular spelling, now rendered gong-fu, literally meaning "accomplishment," a Chinese term used to identify various boxing systems
kyu - category of beginner's rank in training
kyujutsu - Japanese archery
men - head and face covering that makes up a part of the armor in *kendo*
mokuso - meditative sitting
mondo - question and answer session used by Zen masters to lead disciples to enlightenment
montei - disciple
mu-shin - no-mind
nage-waza - throwing techniques of judo and aikido
naginata - a type of halberd used by the samurai
Okinawa-te - traditional term for *karate*
oshiki-uchi - an aiki-jutsu technique

qi - Chinese term for *ki*
quan - Chinese for fist
randori - freedom of action, the judo practice of free fighting
rei - bow
ri - masterful integration of theory with action
ronin - wave man, a masterless samurai
ryu - tradition, the name used to identify a martial arts school
samurai - warrior class of feudal Japan
satori - Sanskrit term for enlightenment
satsujinken - the sword that takes life, part of a motto of Yagyu swordsmen
seishin - spirit
seishin tanren - spiritual forging, the goal of all budo training
seishi o choetsu suru - the action of transcending thoughts of life and death
seiza - formal seated position used for meditation and ceremonial activities in martial arts
sempai - seniors, higher ranking budoka
sensei - teacher
shiai - contest
shihan - master teacher
shinai - mock-sword made of bamboo strips used in modern *kendo*
shinken shobu - literally "real sword contest," a fight to the death
shodan - first *dan*
shogun - military dictator in feudal Japan
shomen - another name for the *kamiza*
sojutsu - medieval Japanese spear technique
suburi - repetitious training of basic strokes in kendo
taekwondo - Korean art analogous to *karate*
tai chi - more formally *tai chi ch'uan* (*tai ji quan*), a Chinese internal system of boxing emphasizing extremely slow movements in set forms
tare - hip protector worn in *kendo*
tatami - mat
te - fist, another term for *karate*

tode - another term for *karate*
tsuki - thrust
waza - a technique
wu-hsing - Chinese phrase for five elements, a school of philosophy
wushu - modern Chinese martial arts, the equivalent of *budo*
yamabushi - mountain warriors, name given to militant disciples of esoteric disciplines
yame - finish, a command used in *karate*
yin/yang - passive and active principles thought to underlie all phenomena
yudansha - *dan* holder, an individual holding a black belt
zanshin - awareness
zarei - formal bow from a seated position
zazen - meditative sitting
Zen - school of Mahayanna Buddhism with a strong influence on martial arts
zendo - Zen training hall

Also Available from Turtle Press:

Teaching: The Way of the Master
Combat Strategy
The Art of Harmony
A Guide to Rape Awareness and Prevention
Total MindBody Training
1,001 Ways to Motivate Yourself and Others
Ultimate Fitness through Martial Arts
Taekwondo Kyorugi: Olympic Style Sparring
Launching a Martial Arts School
Advanced Teaching Report
Hosting a Martial Art Tournament
100 Lost Cost Marketing Ideas for the Martial Arts School
A Part of the Ribbon: A Time Travel Adventure
The Martial Arts Training Diary
The Martial Arts Training Diary for Kids
Neng Da: Super Punches
Martial Arts and the Law
Martial Arts for Women

For more information:
Turtle Press
PO Box 290206
Wethersfield CT 06129-206
1-800-77-TURTL
e-mail: sales@turtlepress.com

http://www.turtlepress.com